D0340365

Also by Jonathan Waterman

*Surviving Denali: A Study of Accidents on
Mt. McKinley*

*High Alaska: A Historical Guide to
Denali, Hunter, and Foraker*

*Cloud Dancers: Portraits of N.A.
Moutaineers* (editor)

*In The Shadow of Denali: Life and Death
on Alaska's Mt. McKinley*

KAYAKING THE VERMILION SEA

Eight Hundred Miles Down the Baja

Jonathan Waterman

SIMON & SCHUSTER
New York London Toronto Sydney Tokyo Singapore

SIMON & SCHUSTER
Rockefeller Center
1230 Avenue of the Americas
New York, NY 10020

SIMON & SCHUSTER and colophon are registered trademarks
of Simon & Schuster Inc.

Designed by Irving Perkins Associates

Manufactured in the United States of America

1   3   5   7   9   10   8   6   4   2

Library of Congress Cataloging-in-Publication Data

Waterman, Jonathan.
Kayaking the Vermilion Sea : eight hundred miles down the Baja / Jonathan
Waterman.
p.   cm.
1. Sea kayaking—Mexico—California, Gulf of. 2. Kayak touring—Mexico—
California, Gulf of. I. Title.
GV788.5.W4 1995
797.1'224164'1—dc20   95-1997
CIP

ISBN 0-684-80242-2

Like pilgrims to the appointed place we tend;
The world's an inn, and death the journey's end.

—JOHN DRYDEN

To Aldo Leopold, John Steinbeck, Joseph Wood Krutch, Ed Abbey, Ann Zwinger, Peter Matthiessen, and Doug Peacock; for sounding the alarm about this sea.

Acknowledgments

My sincere thanks to:

Equipment sponsors: Brunton/Lakota Company—for knives and compasses; Cascade Designs—for sleeping bag and pads; Daiwa Corporation—for fishing gear; Eddyline—for the sea kayaks; Gerber—for knives and fire starter; Kelty—for the tent; Mountain Safety Research—for stove, pots, and dromedary bags; Nike Inc.—for clothing; Patagonia—for sea kayaking clothing; Pur—for filter and desalinator; Sea Wings—for sponsons; Swift Paddles; and Voyageur—for dry bags and paddle gear.

Kiko Callenburger, Dave Kallgren (NOLS), Roy Gillette, Kenneth Norris, Rick Ridgeway, Dix Brow, Michael Bircumshaw (*Baja Sun*), Antonio Cauto Diaz, Becky Aparico and Roy Mayhoff (*Bahía Tropicales*). All provided useful insight.

Western State College librarians, who cheerfully fulfilled sixty-three intralibrary loan requests. The librarians of Crested Butte, Gunnison, and Aspen (Pitkin County) public libraries were also helpful.

Those who read the text and gave me precious advice: Greg Silber of the Marine Mammal Commission and author of *Cetaceans in the Northern Gulf of California;* Paul Konrad, editor of *WildBird* magazine; Ann Zwinger, naturalist and author of *A Desert Country Near the Sea.*

David Hale, Yale Divinity graduate and dilettante hedonist; Susan Golomb, literary agent and trusted advisor; and Mitch Horowitz, Simon & Schuster editor and spiritual coadventurer. Their moral support and camaraderie are my durable ship.

Author's Note

In this book I use the spelling "Cortés" and the acute accent mark employed not only by Hernán Cortés, but found on a sixteenth-century print of him, on a seventeenth-century map of the Sea of Cortés, and used by eminent Mexico historians Francisco Clavijero, William Prescott, and Hugh Thomas. While referring to John Steinbeck's *Log from the Sea of Cortez* and Ray Cannon's *Sea of Cortez,* I use their alternate spelling. The all-but-forgotten "Vermilion Sea" and the modern "Gulf of California" both refer to the Sea of Cortés.

With the exception of using the popular colloquialism "the Baja" in the book's subtitle, I refer to the Mexican peninsula in more recent times as "Baja [Lower] California," and in early days as "California." I call the former Guaycura, Pericú, and Cochimi tribes "Californians." "*Bajacalifornios*" are peninsula dwellers of Mexican citizenship. America's thirty-first state is "Alta [Higher] California."

1

The Weight

Bribing policía—*Why we have come—
Resemblance to the Mediterranean—Is it a mirage?*

Sweat trickles out of my armpits and down my sides until tee shirt and skin become one. Opposite the windshield, the San Felipe Desert sticks to the bleached horizons, while the 103-degree air bends into an ocean of undulating waves. My tongue feels fuzzy, steam hisses from the radiator, and gooey asphalt *click-click-clicks* out of the tires and up into the wheel wells.

Rather than sit in the sweltering cab, Deborah and Jane sprawl in the back of the pickup beneath two sixteen-foot boats. Without their company, I am preoccupied, fidgety, half wishing we had stayed at home; I let my right foot droop until the speedometer wiggles around eighty-five—the age at which I hope to retire.

Behind are two *mas gordo policía* investing our twenty-five-dollar "fine" on *cervezas frías* in the San Luis Cantina—we had broken no laws, but fighting the trumped-up charges at the police station would have taken all day. Easier to put the money on their car seat and race south. If we spend the next two months in border towns, rather than on the Sea of Cortés, we would be fleeced of our money so quickly that we would be tempted, like most gringos, to call Mexicans thieves.

I search the rearview for *policía* as I push my retirement. My wife's image pops into the mirror, scowling, because she is a paramedic and has attended too many highway crashes. I slow down.

We are in Baja Norte, a hundred miles south of the border, and our kayaks are performing like twin aircraft fuselage up in the slipstream above. We are mountain climbers rather than sea kayakers. Hot weather, versus the cool breezes of our home in the Colorado Rockies, withers me. But here is the truth: Deborah and I are bored with ourselves, and it is our custom to abandon our soft lives wherever and however we can. It is our custom to remove ourselves so far from the refrigerator and the couch and the television that we will surprise ourselves with the verity of nerve endings and remnant instincts. It is our custom to find adventure without guides, and in a place where we might glimpse the world not only as the world used to be, but as the world should remain.

I am not happy confined at home. Crested Butte, Colorado, is referred to by locals as "paradise" because of the isolation, the wildflowers, the clear streams, and the flaming aspens fringed by snowcapped mountains. Yet even paradise gets old if you never leave. "To live in one land is captivitie," wrote Donne, "To runne all countries, a wild roguery." Even Darwin observed birds abandoning fledgling chicks in order to satiate the migratory urge. But there is another malaise pressing my shoulders as I steer around a dead dog, stuck to the asphalt as a mat of flies and fur—the fifth dead dog since crossing the border two hours ago. Tires squeal. Deborah's head pops up.

The shortness of life haunts me. Friends get divorced,

species die, disease abounds, people starve, and the autumns become so familiar and sublime that I am no longer admiring the colors of falling leaves so much as aching about their passage. And the cold icon of winter envelops us in the nine-thousand-foot valley we live in; snow fell every month last year.

We have come to Baja California because we want to lighten a ballast. Out among the simplicity of sea and sky I hope to find a way to release this notion that our days are all too short and fragile—this gut feeling that, in the end, life may be worth nothing.

It is all too obvious that most of my friends are unhappy about some similar grimness. We have friends in their forties having heart attacks and brain hemorrhages; no man and woman seem happy together—dozens of local acquaintances split the sheets; and the jokes we laugh loudest at are cynical. Meanwhile, wild places are shrinking and the ozone disappearing and the oceans sludging over as our families and friends grow older and everyone and everything we know eventually dies.

I often wonder if this awareness of life's fragility and suffering—the Buddhists call it *duhkha*—is what sends people to cynicism, drugs, alcohol, or religion.

Henry David Thoreau wrote that we *should go to* the wilderness, rather than *escape from* the rest of our lives. Although I have always tried to realize that maxim, I can no longer deny the need to escape. Immersing myself into adventure, into wilderness, is a means to confront, or lessen, the weight of life.

If the gnashing of tectonic plates had spun Mexico another ninety degrees, the Sea of Cortés would appear on maps as a bantam Mediterranean. In 1602, Father Antonio de la Ascensión sailed west across the sea:

> It is but fifty leagues [125 miles] across the Mediterranean Sea of California, which others call "Mar Rojo"

[Sea Red] from the Islas de Mazatlán to this point. This sea, as I have explained in other places, extends to the Strait of Anian by which there is a communication with the ocean of the north. It contains in itself much riches and on its coast on both sides there are many pearl beds, and in the mountains very rich mines of gold and silver, and there is much amber.

The Mediterranean's Naples, Monte Carlo, Sicily, and Corsica resemble mainland Mexico's Guaymas and Mazatlán, as well as the islands of Tiburón and Ángel de la Guarda. Its desert shore, Baja California, evokes the barren shores of North Africa. The twenty-three-hundred-mile-long Mediterranean has browned with pollution, and now the seven-hundred-mile-long Sea of Cortés is degrading. The good news? The Sea of Cortés remains the richest body of water on the planet. Amid Pacific tidal surges that rake the sea over deep ocean trenches rife with plankton, there are over eight hundred marine vertebrates and two thousand spineless life forms, eclipsing even the former Mediterranean's glory.

Nonetheless, Mexican waters appear bound for the same microbial bankruptcy as the Mediterranean. At the head of the sea, the formerly nutrient-rich Colorado River has been plugged dry, just as the Aswan Dam denied the Nile's nutrients to the Mediterranean. Mexican shrimp trawlers, foreign fishing fleets, and, to a lesser extent, sportfishing tourists are in danger of fishing the sea to the same depletion of southern Europe. And hotels, condominiums, and homes are inundating the Baja California dunes like the south of France.

Amid this coming tsunami of development, we are no different from anyone else: Deborah and I want to explore this Garden of Eden before the water becomes sterilized and blue-tinted. We're here because the Mediterranean is sanitized and we want to paddle upon waters still teeming with life.

Since I cannot stomach the countless interviews, barhopping, Montezuma's Revenge, and debilitating peninsula highway driving that most journalists would submit themselves to, we will perform our research "immersion style." Paddling for two months and living off the sea should show us, firsthand, the state of Hernán Cortés's namesake.

Three years ago, Deborah and I came to this sea only as lovers, but after ten days alone together in kayaks, we became as close as two people can be. Since then we have repeatedly fantasized of returning and paddling the entire sea. The 1990 jaunt was a reference point in our lives, a time of innocence and discovery that we want to revisit. In the recesses of our subconscious we cling to a theology that something awaits us at journey's end, perhaps an understanding with one another, or a way to once and for all shed this misunderstood and cumbersome weight.

The kayaks catch air up on the jury-rigged ski racks: whooshing up, creaking against the climbing ropes lashed above, and thumping the roof upon their descent. Deborah's eyes become slits as she grabs a paddle to poke me.

Cresting a rise, the sea suddenly appears to the east. Everything changes. Where we were once listless commuters, our lives are suddenly filled with mission and meaning; I rein in my retirement foot and let the speedometer drop back down around my age: thirty-seven. Upon his first eyeful of the Pacific Ocean, William Clark (accompanying Meriwether Lewis) exclaimed, "O! the joy!"—exactly my sentiments.

The frenzy of making a living, and the falseness of speeding south on melting asphalt for three days, makes the brilliant specter to our left appear unspoiled. *Where else?* I ask myself. Here, as Melville once wrote, is a sweet mystery that speaks of some hidden soul beneath. We stare as if it is chimera galloping along the horizon. I squint for a different view because there is the indelible impression that the water is moving, that the sea is actually alive. Even the early explorers called it the Vermilion Sea (Mar Bermejo) for vast shrimp hatches and untold plains of microscopic life reddening the waters.

This infinite aqueous plain mirrors the sun as if we are staring into the dazzling topaz eye of God—and It just winked. I blink my own eyes, slowly, just to ascertain that the sea is not a mirage.

2

From Castle Peak, We Fall to the Sea

My wife and me—Defining a journey—How stingrays jerk—
What we carry—The Outward Bound disaster—
A checklist of alluring hazards

Those who compete with my wife running, skiing, or biking call her "An Engine." Here on the San Felipe beach, she lugs fourteen gallons of drinking water down to the waterline, then a duffel filled with ten days of pasta and dried food. I fiddle with the knotted kayaks on the pickup roof.

Deborah's blond hair falls to her shoulders. Her triceps and quadriceps are the sort of sleekly defined muscles known as "slow twitch"—metabolizing oxygen at a rate that enhances long-term endurance. She has blue-tiled-swimming-pool-colored eyes. If someone upsets Deborah, she narrows those eyes until colorless, arches her black eyebrows, and usually gets an apology without asking. She is thirty-five years old. Deborah came to Mexico once before, taking time off from Middlebury College and the National Nordic racing team to live with a wealthy Mexican businessman across the sea.

She recently left her job as director of Crested Butte's Emergency Medical Services. She couldn't take answering the phone at all hours, working with scantily trained volunteers, and being on call seven days a week. While trying to figure out what will make her happy, Deborah continues working the ambulance in her hometown, Aspen.

She has learned how to save lives. If victims don't make it, Deborah wrestles with her emotions until she finds a way to bury the grimness of trauma. She believes that helping others is one way to lighten this load that we carry. Sometimes, however, she comes home spent from a twenty-four-hour shift after tending to a hopeless crash or abused children and then the world's gravity comes down so hard that she'll cry and we'll hold one another tightly and try to talk but most of the time she has no choice but to move on. Most of the time when she finishes a bad shift I'm not around, or I don't have the right words to help her, so she'll slip into her sneakers and run for a couple hours in the mountains, lithe as a deer fleeing bullets.

A year ago, climbing to our wedding above Aspen and Crested Butte, we raced one another up. On top of Castle Peak (14,265 feet) the minister and we were veiled by passing clouds, tickling snow squalls, and saffron beams of high-altitude sun. We recited North American Indian folklore, Chinese philosophy, and old English verse. We slipped rings on our fingers and our horizon merged into a limitless sea of possibilities to be explored.

Although I flip past newspaper horoscope pages, Deborah gave me a book about our mutual birthsign. The chapter about our marriage reads: "If Gemini expects to establish a stable, mature environment with its twin, it could be disappointed. Such a partnership can sometimes resemble a swordfight." The chapter concludes: "A Gemini is more than a bargain to its twin partner—it will be a treasure whose worth is beyond calculation."

Inside my ring, Deborah had engraved an etching of Denali (Mount McKinley), where I had spent a decade guiding, rangering, and living near the mountain. So in the spring we climbed Denali and the trip freed Deborah from ambulance work. We zipped our sleeping bags together against thirty-below-zero temperatures. We roped together for thirty-six days and performed for the cameras—the hardest expedition of nearly thirty climbs for me because of our quarreling and our competitive relationship.

I came away with new respect for her psychological strength while waiting out a week of subzero storm at seventeen thousand feet. Her endurance amazed the male film crew—professional guides and climbers. She has all the broad-faced radiance and sensitive acuity of a feminine cover girl, but an unbending will makes capitulation difficult; this, in part, is why I love my wife.

While returning from Alaska to Crested Butte, casting about for the next adventure, I suggested that we try and paddle the Northwest Passage in the Arctic. Deborah's freckles darkened while her face blanched icy white. "C'mon," she said, "we spend all our time surrounded by winter. Let's go back to the Baja where it's warm."

I agreed immediately. The only obstacle was finding someone to rent our house and take care of our geriatric dog, Molly. It is not always easy for husband and wife to work closely with one another, and adventure trips only introduce more rough sailing to the already roiled waters of marriage.

Whether married or single, I have long perceived the ocean as a place that holds that same limitless fascination, mystery, and challenge that mountains have always seduced me with. The English author and explorer, H. W. Tilman, waited until he was fifty years old and standing heavy-footed beneath Everest before concluding that sailing might be a better avocation—but life should have smoother transitions. Once my joints start calcifying, I'll trade a sea kayak for a sailboat.

Finding as many unexploited pieces of earth as Tilman did sixty years ago is tough. But only during a journey, by suffering (slightly) and solving wilderness obstacles, can I separate myself from the homebound stasis of gathering information and pecking upon the keyboard.

Journeys are partly about getting back in touch with your own muscle fiber, growing thin while eating all the time, and becoming abstemious of the temptations at home. The bad part of journeys is the urge to go from point A to point B as fast as you can. Competitive challenge and physical demand blurs the natural world. Even worse, by going quickly we would merely flee that *weight,* that fragility we are trying to come to terms with. So my philosophy is to go slowly.

A woman who paddled from San Felipe to La Paz with her husband told me that they took twenty-six days to paddle over six hundred miles—a new record. I asked about fishing; she didn't fish. I asked if she tried to sail; she paddled. And I asked if they spent time with Mexicans; "no time," she replied. It was as if they had maxed out the mileage meter on the rowing machine at the health club. We allowed two months for our own slightly longer journey.

Deborah and I heft the sixty-pound kayaks off the roof, one at a time, and walk them to the water; I set my end down as gently as if returning it to mother in the maternity ward. Then we hug Jane good-bye. She is stanching her tears as she confronts south-of-the-border rumors about lone American women and corrupt *policía.* We have offered to drive Jane back, but the logistics seem insurmountable, so she bravely returns north alone. In broad daylight, on a busy highway, she'll be fine.

Between stuffing waterproof bags into the front and rear compartments of our kayaks, we jump into the sea, which is twenty degrees cooler than the triple-digit air temperatures. We float with eyes closed, pedaling our hands like sea lions, exposing only our faces to hot air.

We shuffle—instead of stepping—across the sea bottom to scare off half-buried stingrays. One flick of a stingray's barbed tail into a human leg ruptures a thin sheath on the tail and daubs venom into the victim's wound; the jagged teeth of this barb widen the wound when the stingray jerks back its tail. However, since the venom is heat labile, soaking your foot in hot water counteracts the fever, nausea, vomiting, or arrhythmia.

For our bodies, we carry a ten-pound medical kit. It is stuffed with morphine ampules, demerol, several courses of antibiotics, anti-inflammatories, sutures, scissors, narcotics, medical tape, gauze, Ben-Gay, hemorrhoid cream, eye ointment, Band-Aids, ten tubes of sun cream, fifty Pepto-Bismol tablets, and enough hard candy to keep our mouths from drying out in the desert.

For the mind, we carry twenty pounds of books. Five flora and fauna guidebooks, along with another dozen fiction and nonfiction narratives.

For thirst, if we should run out of drinking water, we carry a desalinator that will make a liter of water after forty minutes of vigorous pumping. We don't carry toilet paper or anything else that we can't carry out.

Toilet paper is the one sure sign of human intervention in the wilderness. Deborah and I have seen "bowel prayer flags" flying from the mountains of Alaska to the beaches of Thailand. Toilet paper fluttering across pristine sections of the earth is not the earth's worst environmental atrocity, but it may be the most prevalent. It can be buried, or burned, but coyotes and other hungry animals have a knack for unearthing used toilet paper. Sailors simply flush it into the ocean, while purists carry it out—a messy situation for long trips. So we only use it at home. Employing a bit of imagination about natural substitutes for toilet paper, and a bit more discretion about shape and texture—clam shells, for instance, are preferable over conches—hygienic travelers don't have to revert to aborigines.

We don't carry a radio or an emergency locator beacon even though the sea is renowned for disasters. In January 1978, nine Outward Bound students paddled out into a building north wind, late in the morning. It was a mistake. Dawn departures are the best chance of avoiding these afternoon winds that put the fear of God into anyone piloting a boat smaller than a twin-diesel cabin cruiser.

The winds gusted to fifty miles per hour and the Outward Bound kayaks swamped. Unlike most boats, a loaded kayak places you slightly below the water and even a four-foot wave looms over your head and intimidates you. According to the survivors, the waves were fifteen feet high. And the shore was cliffed. They had no choice but to tie their half-capsized boats together into a big raft and hold on for their lives while shivering in sixty-degree water.

Brenda Herman, twenty years old, and David Schwimmer, eighteen—already weakened from dysentery—were blown away from the group and drowned. The remaining seven students clung to their rafted kayaks most of the night, until Timothy Breidegam, twenty-one, couldn't hold on any longer and drowned. Eventually the six survivors washed ashore.

They walked for two days before flagging down a passing fisherman. Schwimmer's body was probably eaten by sharks, while Breidegam's and Herman's bodies were found washed ashore two days later.

The media accounts would have us believe that they were killed by a savage sea. During ensuing lawsuits, the parents claimed that Outward Bound was guided by reckless philosophy. Deborah and I could also paddle into the north winds or a *chubasco* (hurricane from the mainland), then get swamped by waves too big to paddle; so out in a potential firing zone like this, we pay attention. Safe journeys can also be defined by a constant reduction of risks; by clutching *respect* for the sea—by admitting fear and showing deference and feeling awe—we effectively plan our survival.

Listening to that remnant voice of instinct helps too. If you're out for more than a few weeks, you can come to know the wilds with the same explicit sensuality as your spouse, you can close your eyes and *feel* the mood of a place, and you can actually sense danger. This instinctive "radar" has kept me out of avalanches, crevasses, and storms; without "listening" to it I would have died by now. Although there is little science about the reliability of human instinct, the cognoscenti of adventuring listen to it; neophytes often substitute avalanche transceivers, radios, search beacons, and expensive technologic equipment for instinct. Adventurers too busy listening to technology often don't "hear" their own instincts.

We have also been warned about rattlesnakes dozing under sleeping bags, neuro-toxic sea snakes curling under kayaks, scorpions crawling into shoes, seventeen-foot-wide manta rays jumping out of the water and capsizing kayaks, whirlpools forming out of the tides, *elefante* winds blowing small boats out to sea, and tarantulas nesting as copiously as ground squirrels. We are also wary of stepping on poisonous sea urchin spines, getting between a killer whale calf and a protective mother, encountering thirty-eight different species of shark, dehydrating along the many arid desert sections, meeting foul-tempered sea lion bulls, and developing crippling paddler's tendinitis.

While at home, struck by the notion that stasis can be cured by adventure, these hazards seemed alluring. From our mountain-climbing perspective, these hazards also seemed novel. Deborah and I reassured ourselves that if the peninsula lacked fangs and the sea was the Mediterranean, it wouldn't be the *real* wilderness adventure we need to pull ourselves and our marriage together. Even Odysseus would have chosen to stay home and gather rust rather than to weigh anchor in a sea without Cyclops. This is how we thought at home. But while standing calf deep in the sea beside a loaded kayak trying to remember what we forgot and how we will cope with the next eight hundred miles, the bottom falls out of my stomach and my mouth tastes of tin.

3

The Architect's Work

Pelicans and cormorants—Sebastián Vizcaíno in 1602—The discomfort of a sea kayak—Digging a grave—Rising full moon

We shove off at midafternoon, hoping to find a deserted beach to sleep on, anything but the town of San Felipe. It's not Mexico when Americans outnumber Mexicans on the streets. Our kayaks carve smoothly through an afternoon chop, but I stop frequently and plunge my arms elbow deep in the turquoise waters to cool my blistering palms.

Fishermen pass us constantly in their wake-producing *pangas*—like Boston whalers—and the outboard fuel stings my nostrils. *Pangas* are festively painted or left in dull white according to the whims of their owners. The boats are purchased from an American out of La Paz; Malcolm Shroyer foresaw the fishing industry and built a boat that fast-forwarded the local economy. Since the 1970s, Shroyer has replaced Baja California's former canoes carved out of logs with these fiberglass *pangas,* designed with buoyant bows for lifting through the swell. The beefed-up stern holds hundred-horsepower outboards—which are expensive, but fishermen are cashy in a good season. The lightweight boats move like corvettes, hydroplaning through miles of troubling chop and contrary current.

Deborah shrinks into the distance. Her lithe arms appear as pistons: pushing and pulling on the double-bladed paddle with machinelike efficiency. With no hope of catching up to her, I hover at the entrance to a rock breakwater that stinks finer than a fish market. Shrimp trawlers peeling paint-jobs fold into the sea.

A brown pelican silently brakes from its thirty-mile-per-hour flight, wheeling above me, crashing seaward. The bird swallows a mouthful of smelt, cracking like an unfurling flag. It swims off at about three miles per hour, fast as I can paddle. In 1602, Sebastián Vizcaíno sailed around Lower California and described brown pelicans:

> Here those of the Almiranta went ashore, particularly Father Antonio who, in company with Captain Peguero went looking all over it. In one place they

found a pelican with a broken wing tied, and around
him many little piles of fresh fish, and of good large
sardines which the other pelicans had brought him to
eat as he could not catch them by reason of his cap-
tivity and disability, so merciful are these birds. . . .
This was a device of the Indians to sustain themselves
with dry feet, because when they saw plenty of fish
around the captive pelican, they came out of ambush,
frightened the birds away and gathered up what was
there, going back to hide again, and waiting for them
to bring more. In this way the Indians obtained quite
sufficient fish without greater labor (secret wisdom of
God that we may praise Him in His works and mar-
vels). Father Antonio out of compassion released the
pelican and let him go free to the water.

Three hundred and sixty years later, pesticides nearly
wiped out brown pelicans in California. Although Mexican pelican eggs within three hundred miles of the border were also
thin from levels of DDE (a component of DDT), the lack of pesticides on the peninsula—along with the abundance of herring,
sardines, and anchovies in the sea—offered a refuge for the
species. DDT was outlawed in the United States and *Pelecanus
occidentalis* was taken off the endangered species list in 1973.

After paddling another hour, I feel stuffed into my kayak
casing, but my competitive wife is still in sight and the shoreline steadily unrolls southward, like the script in a player piano.
A long-necked cormorant watches me warily before diving
amid schools of yellow-purple-orange fish skittering below. I
plunge my arms into turquoise coolness. Forty seconds later
the cormorant surfaces ninety yards to seaward, quiet as a
snake.

After two hours, the fiberglass kayak braces have im-
printed my legs. I plunge my arms in and fantasize of a quick
cooling Eskimo roll, the virtuoso method of uncapsizing. Although I can perform a marginal roll in an empty river kayak,

190 pounds of food, fuel, water, and gear would hobble even a seasoned kayaker. Besides, my waterproof spray skirt—which draws tight around the cockpit and under one's armpits—is too deeply buried. I settle for splashing sea in my face.

At dusk, twelve *pangas* roar north of San Felipe. The rotten egg smell of trash burning over someone's dinner fire hangs like a storm cloud over the local vicinity, and undoubtably, most of Mexico.

We pull ashore with our fiberglass hulls grating and scraping against the sandpaper beach. A sign, VEHÍCULOS PROHIBATO EN LA PLAYA, reads that the fine for beach driving on this half mile of protected dunes is one hundred dollars. Camping here is our best bet against a dune buggy flattening us in our sleep.

A puppy is curled in the sand. Under the saffron light the puppy appears more alive than dead, glowing just like my own arms under the moonlight. The carcass is long enough picked by the crabs and baked by the sun that the decayed odor of death is almost gone. I dig a grave with my hands, then scoop sand over bared teeth. I would like to shrug this encounter off, and by acting as if I never saw the dead dog, I might forget it, at least consciously. Instead, I contemplate more pleasant destinations: maybe an expensive resort in the Caribbean. Certainly Disney World. Maybe even Paris. Here in Mexico's Sea of Cortés, however, six dead dogs in two days seems a bad omen. Deborah is crying. We hug one another tightly. "Honey," I whisper all earnest in her ear, "it could be worse. At least we're on vacation."

She stops crying, wipes her face, and confronts me, "This trip will *not* be a vacation, Jonathan."

When you're single, it's tempting to hammer out arguments; but when you're married, the best tool is to hug your partner when you disagree. Even if you're right. Especially if you're wrong. After all, to me adventures *are* a vacation; to her (she gets mail from a dozen animal rights groups), this is like journeying through an evil cosmetic company's test kennels. She's scared about the puppy and anxious about what lies ahead so she is venting emotionally. I hug her and say, "Welcome to Mexico, honey," and watch the light outside.

As the sun drops below the sand dunes, the south wind drops. The sea falls to slack tide and sighs against the mud and sand shore effluent of the Colorado River. Within this seemingly haphazard architecture of earth, wind, sea, and sky beside the puppy grave, it is easy to believe that there are no plans. The sun drops lower and an unseen and gargantuan cloud casts a clearly defined black beam above the Sea of Cortés. This hundred-mile shadow glows against the sky as the sea breathes in and out. More respirations pass as Deborah and I clutch one another on our muddy sand floor.

Only the earth's unspoiled cornucopias can seem to invert shadows into beams of light. Who can say why such animal-intensive shelters as the Arctic National Wildlife Refuge, the Serengeti, or the Sea of Cortés have the finest natural light. Does the proliferation of animals come first, as in the process of photosynthesis? Or does shadow and light attract wildlife as it has drawn us?

As if to answer our questions, the shadow disappears with the suddenness of a flipped light switch. Then a guttural bird croaking arises from our front yard and the full moon rises as large as the day, profiling a great blue heron fishing stilt-legged in the water. A flashing school of mullets plops back into the silver sea; two coyotes sing in symphony; a mouse darts beneath our feet.

This is the hand of the Architect.

4

The Sea's Lungs

How the tide moves—Colorado River Delta—A rattling by
the tent door—Needlefish—1,080,000 paddle strokes

By eight at night—if such a vibrant moon wouldn't qualify this
as daytime—the Sea of Cortés has fallen a hundred yards from
our tent. We exhale as the ocean continues to breathe in.

We stroll above the water picking up shells and measuring
with our toes two-foot-wide scoops made by stingrays. We are
fifteen feet lower than the frothy leavings of high tide. The
night is silent, approaching the slack between tides, and we
can almost hear the sea breathing if we hold our breath and listen to it caressing the shore: a tossed sheet settling on a bed.

The moon's gravity accounts for today's "spring" tide—the
Saxon *springan* means "rising" or "welling." In another fourteen days, when the new moon is a sliver in the sky, there will
be an even higher rise, a lower ebb. Our own fluid bodies, our
moods and our menses, are similarly controlled by these cos-

mic forces. I can plan on a reanimation, the giddy euphoria
that full moons provoke in me.

Although a marine biologist wouldn't try to personify this
supposedly inanimate ocean, we like to imagine that aqueous
bodies are vitalized by microorganisms and the moon. Our
bodies are filled with swimming platelets, bacteria, and all
number of creatures, just like the sea. We breathe in, the ocean
breathes out.

These heavily sedimented northern waters are no deeper
than 650 feet. Two tides a day sweep through the twenty-six-
hundred-foot-deep midriff (a hundred miles south), carrying
plankton, fish, and oxygen to a myriad of marine life.

Two tides a day create three- to five-mile-per-hour currents, which will present us with the most challenging paddling
of our journey. In kayaks, however, when the currents pull too
heavy, we will take out and wait for a slack tide. Yachts or
cruising boats can't pull out or anchor in the places that we'll
drag our kayaks into, nor would large boats want to trifle with
the currents of the northern gulf. Fine by us: we like being
alone.

In 1539, Francisco de Ulloa felt an incalculable isolation
when he became the first to sail up the sea. Aside from a few
scattered tribes of Indians, the peninsula was an arid wilderness. He named the sea Mar de Cortés after his gold-and-pearl-
driven commander. Sailing to the shallow head of the gulf, he
found the river he named Colorado for the redness of its clay-
blanketed waters. Ulloa wrote:

> We found a channel two leagues from the mainland,
> eight fathoms deep, into which its two tides flooded
> every twenty-four hours in their order, flood and ebb,
> without falling off a jot and with a flood and an ebb
> current so strong that it was marvelous. When the tide
> ran out it left dry, and when it flooded it covered
> more than two leagues [five miles] which lay between
> where we were and the mainland.

Prior to the construction of the Hoover Dam, the Colorado River clashed with the sea's tides and formed walls of water comparable to Nova Scotia's Bay of Fundy. A Mexican steamer flipped over in this tidal bore, which claimed eighty lives; other boats were wrecked, lost anchors, or foundered on the extensive tidal flats. In 1857, Joseph Ives of the United States Army Engineers wrote:

> A great wave, several feet in height, could be distinctly seen flashing and sparkling in the moonlight, extending from one bank to the other, and advancing swiftly upon us . . . the broad sheet around us boiled up and foamed like the surface of a cauldron, and then, with scarcely a moment of slack water, the whole went whirling by . . . with the thunder of a cataract.

After steaming for two days upriver, to the region of today's Hoover Dam, Ives underestimated the capacity of his employer: "The Colorado River, along the greater portion of its lonely and majestic way, shall be forever unvisited and undisturbed."

The Colorado River used to carry down half of the sea's freshwater, along with some 165 million metric tons of sediment each year, coating the sea bottom three miles thick. After the Hoover Dam's construction in 1935, these sediments— never mind the freshwater with its life-sustaining nitrates and phosphates—no longer reach the sea.

Although we are here by virtue of the technology that made dams, shaped our fiberglass kayaks, invented the reverse-osmosis desalinator, and allowed us to drive fifty miles past the muddy delta, my chest constricts with this arbitration against nature. The river is damned, the northern dunes are overrun, and the sea is losing its life blood.

• • •

Scores of ghost crabs scuttle as eight-legged penlights in front of our feet and disappear into holes above the darkened waterline. I step up to the tent, but a buzzing like that from a low-frequency beehive prevents me from taking the last step. A rattlesnake is coiled and ready to strike, guarding the door; I jump back; Deborah screams. Under my headlamp beam, its eyes glow as orange bonfires, its tongue flickers for our scent, its buzzing tail waves ominously. I feel an urge to kill the snake—partly so we don't get bitten, and partly for food. I ask Deborah if she has ever eaten rattlesnake and her gasp of incredulity makes me ashamed for even suggesting it. A few gentle flips with a kayak paddle send the rattler away.

Surely we can sleep untroubled in the tent—free of snakes, scorpions, or crabs. Free of evening news, ringing telephone, or broken gas heater. But the knowledge that technology has prevented a vast river from clashing with the sea, the knowledge that I am not separate from the dam, makes me toss and turn for hours. I wonder if it is innately human to try and dominate the natural world—for in my desire to kill the snake, am I the same as those who killed the river?

As I close my eyes, I breathe out. Before I drift off, the sea breathes in.

At nine in the morning—we're too tired to leave at dawn— we're wakened by a backpacker returning to San Felipe. Inspired by Graham Mackintosh's book about walking three thousand miles around the peninsula, our morning visitor had hoped to do the same. He has blisters, he can't carry enough water to slake his thirst, and his brand-new yellow pack and stiff-looking leather boots betray his inexperience. Here beside the vastness of the sea, despite scattered cottages and passing dune buggies, there is a spatial solitude that can drive you deaf if you can't communicate with it. As he waves good-bye, headed home to Texas, we admire his attempt: better to fail than dream impotently. But Deborah's silence accentuates my thinking: *Have we also gotten in over our heads?*

Most kayakers pick their coveted boats off the ground and carry them to the water, but since the sea has moved out a half mile, we drag our half-loaded boats like mules to briny water. It takes three trips to lug the rest of our gear down. In the elapsed forty minutes, we must pull the boats another forty yards to catch the receding waters. Until we pass the midriff, where the tides drop a mere three feet, our existence will hinge upon the push and pull of the moon.

When we round a sandy point, twelve egrets, thirty-two pelicans, and an uncountable gang of western gulls stand in the rank and file of their own kind, each separated by ten yards. Their heads turn south as we paddle by, Deborah bidding good morning to each species.

After a few minutes of paddling I'm covered with a sheen of sweat. The sun pours down like molten honey and I try to shrink under my ball cap for more shade. Three-foot-long bar-

racudalike needlefish plop in front of our bows. I was once lucky enough to spear a pipe-shaped, crocodile-beaked needlefish—*Tylosurus crocodilus.* Because of its neon green bones and flesh, the needlefish is unlikely to become the marketable commodity that most other creatures in the sea have been relegated to.

In Los Barriles, the southern windsurfing mecca of the peninsula, hitting needlefish is no joke. One windsurfing local, sailing along at forty miles per hour, was drilled through his calf by a jumping needlefish. Another windsurfer kneed a jumping needlefish and needed surgical reconstruction.

Deborah jokingly suggests that I don a spray skirt in case one of the sharp-toothed needlefish jumps into my open cockpit. *Crocodilus* would flop around scissoring scores of needle-sharp teeth near my crotch and although I would try and flip it out of the boat, no telling what its teeth might snag.

My legs chafe from the braces. My feet cramp on the rudder pedals. My rear end aches from the plastic seat. And my upper neck grates from the paddling.

Seventy pelicans line up on one beach, waiting for the morning tide to come in. Hundreds of anchovies writhe just under the surface in a twenty-foot-wide, green blurred ball. A dozen pompano clear the water in synchronized arcs, frightened by our porpoise-shaped boats. An osprey flies inland clutching something in its talons.

As we pull further away from San Felipe, the drone of *pangas* recedes. The passing shoreline unveils a couple of hotels, several building projects, and numerous cottages or *campos,* accessed by pavement somewhere beyond the dunes. Gringos and Mexicans frolic in the water and picnic on the beach; three-wheelers and dune buggies whine back and forth.

Every hour we slip our paddles into the shock-corded deck rigging and sip water from polyethylene bottles. Every two hours, we pull ashore on quiet sand beaches to stretch our legs. After nearly five hours of paddling, a rhythm comes—albeit a begrudging rhythm—more like the giddy, singsong flow of my body producing epinephrine than any sort of paddle music. Envisioning the paddle as a cello bow, my left paddle blade strums a note underwater as my right blade describes a lazy arc toward the sky. I brace with thighs and feet, and use my back to push, rather than pull toward our destination eight hundred miles south. Sixty notes a minute; thirty-six hundred notes an hour; twenty-two hundred notes a day. One million and eighty thousand notes will play a symphonic journey's end.

The tide kisses high on the peninsula, the pelicans start diving again, and we begin looking for a secluded white-sand beach.

The bows lift out of the incoming waves, keeping us dry, and slapping gently back into the troughs. Errant breaking waves are parted by the peaked-angle decks, instead of flooding into our cockpits. Nonetheless, if it gets any rougher, we'll be sealing ourselves in the cockpits with our elasticized spray skirts. Unlike the wide, smooth swells of the Pacific, the Sea of Cortés is renowned for short-radius, bumpy chop, distinctly unsettling in a cabin cruiser, but invigorating from our perspective. We're just kids playing in the surf.

Once I find the rhythm to this chop, a flash of cool insight washes over me. I have come to the Sea of Cortés for its newness. As adults, so much of our lives and work are necessarily old and familiar, which is advantageous in terms of our security, productivity for our employers, and our fragile egos. But precious time passes so quickly when life is old and familiar. The days fly by as we dispatch our money to the bill collectors and make the same old pilgrimage to the grocery store, the same old visit to the doctor, and regret the same old passage of the short weekend. Even society regales time by celebrating the young, who have plenty of time, and ignoring the elderly, who have none. At home, time definitely conspires against me—even though I am not yet gray and I am one of those lucky people who does not mind hard work and who occasionally laughs and plays like a child.

The last two days in the Sea of Cortés have passed like a month. We ogle new sunrises, admire new fish, marvel at each new shell, and walk in the moonlight. Of course, the paddling sometimes seems to go on forever, but the *newness* of Oceania slows everything down and makes me feel each moment more intensely, as if I were a child learning about this new world with bright, wonder-filled eyes.

I come out of my reverie and test my insight with the real world as three fins bounce playfully through the water directly toward me. I have no fear. They're dolphins. I stick my hand under water and offer my palm to them as a gesture of submission and friendship. It seems to take forever for the three dolphins—who knows what species—to pass under my boat. Although they won't allow me to touch their soft and porcelain-smooth backs, we look into one another's eyes and discover a kinship that shrinks the universe, distorts time, and tightens my skin.

5

Handout to the Little Cow

*Mammals of the sea—Vaquita porpoise—The lumbering
totoaba—Endangered species protection—Pressing interests
of a hungry country*

The dolphins diving below my hand are members of the mammal order Cetacea, which includes whales and porpoises. Although they appear to be grinning, the flared, friendly-looking lower jawbone on dolphins acts as an ear to detect the high-frequency whistles of fellow cetaceans. Each dolphin has a distinctive whistle that allows a family to know its members' whereabouts without actually seeing them, and to whistle various information to one another. *Look out!* they could be whistling. *Don't touch that hand.*

Of the sixty-five species of dolphins (not to be confused with the game fish dorado, or dolphinfish), nine wander the Sea of Cortés. The gentle-eyed dolphins below have the same memory capacity as I, and undoubtably they will not allow me to touch their soft backs because they have not forgotten their abuse and the previous deaths of family members at the hands of other humans, in similar *panga*-sized boats, wielding gill nets.

We guess that these three are bottlenose dolphins because of their proximity to the shoreline; common dolphins are found in larger schools and further out from shore. Both species are among the most intelligent mammals, and while tuna netting and shrimp trawling has reduced cetacean populations around the world—thousands of dolphins and porpoises are killed each year by fishermen—their continued existence is somewhat assured because of the recent ban on dolphin-killing tuna fish companies. Baja Mexico has had mammal comebacks: the formerly endangered gray whale population recovered after whale hunting was banned. But on a worldwide scale, most cetacean populations have dropped: the right whale, the Indus River dolphin, the baiji dolphin, the black dolphin, and the most endangered of them all: the vaquita porpoise.

The vaquita (little cow) is found only in the Sea of Cortés. It can live for twenty-one years (two-thirds that of bottlenose dolphins), grows to just under five feet, and does not exceed 105 pounds—one-third the weight of most dolphins. Unlike dolphins, the six species of porpoise do not have elongated beaks; the vaquita, identified by a curved dorsal fin and black eye patches, does not play in the bow waves of boats. Most sightings are more than six miles out, and only in the northern sea.

Vaquitas "talk" in order to interpret their narrow confines. Although they do not whistle like dolphins, the higher frequency "clicks" are undetectable by sharks and killer whales. By short, focused bursts, these echoing sonar clicks pare out bottom reverberations or shrimp clicking, and are used to find food—bottom fish, squid, and crabs—deaf to high frequencies. This sonar talk allows the vaquita to use the murky waters of the shallow, northern sea as camouflage against predator and prey.

According to several different censuses, the vaquita population has dwindled as low as three hundred. The species reproduces once a year and from necropsies performed on forty vaquitas drowned in fishing nets, many ovaries contained calcified growths, meaning no babies. Of these recovered carcasses, all are under three or over ten years old. This "age structure breakdown" is seen in the road maps of biology as a warning sign because a lack of all or many age classes is read by biologists as the coming crash of a species—no different from those signs exhibited by the totoaba (an endangered fish residing only in the Sea of Cortés), the Mexican wolf, the passenger pigeon, and the stellar sea cow.

Mammalogists theorize that the vaquita's ancestor was the Burmeister's porpoise, now found off the coast of Peru (and eaten by Peruvians). During the last ice age, this porpoise swam several thousand miles north, through the cooled waters of the tropics, becoming trapped by a system of sills and ledges in the northern Sea of Cortés. Over the years vaquitas coped with the warmer temperatures of the northern sea by evolving into smaller, more energy-efficient animals, and by retaining large, heat dissipating flippers and fins (the largest dorsal fin per body size of any cetacean).

No porpoise is as small as the vaquita. Nor is there another cetacean inhabiting a mere two thousand square miles of increasingly saline sea, harbored against a broken, pesticide toilet of a river.

The population of the vaquita might have numbered several thousand before the damming of the Colorado and before every foot of the northern sea was raked over by shrimp trawlers twice a year. But there is precious little science on *Phocoena sinus* (porpoise of the gulf), given that fossil remains of porpoises are at least 11 million years old and given that the vaquita was not discovered by a scientist until the same summer as my own relatively recent birth in 1956.

Nearly a decade later, vaquita remains began turning up on other Sea of Cortés beaches. American and Mexican scientists began to calculate threats to the vaquita: the dried up Colorado River caused increased salinity and a lack of nutrients; the lightweight and durable monofilament fishing nets, first introduced in Mexico in the 1950s, were taking a toll on many species.

The vaquita's demise became linked to the lumbering fish called the totoaba. Both species are endemic to the Sea of Cortés. Evidence shows that freshwater is essential for incubating the totoaba's eggs, laid each spring in the Colorado River delta. The demise of this fish, which grows to six feet long and three hundred pounds, is also connected with its tender and tastier-than-bass appeal in foreign fish markets. In 1942, the totoaba catch was 2,261 metric tons. The catches decreased incrementally as more dams were built and more gill nets employed. By 1975 only fifty-eight tons were caught. The same two-inch-wide nets that hooked the totoaba's gills and prevented them from backing out hooked the fins of the vaquita and drowned them. Funnel-shaped, shrimp trawler nets also caught totoabas, vaquitas, and any other sea creatures—pulled up onto the deck to die until these unmarketable "trash fish" are shoveled back into an area where the trawlers wouldn't re-catch them. Scientists estimate that nearly forty vaquitas (15 to 20 percent of the population) are accidentally caught and killed by fishermen each year.

PESCA, the Federal Department of Fisheries, imposed a ban on totoaba fishing. But limited enforcement agencies were working in an awfully big sea, and Mexican fishermen have to eat. The ban, in fact, created a pricey black market for totoaba, while even more gill nets were set for sharks and manta rays— the new rage in United States and Japanese fish markets. In 1978, the International Union of Nature and Natural Resources listed the vaquita as a "vulnerable species"; a Mexican mammalogist included the vaquita on a list of rare and endangered species.

In recent years, thirty-two vaquitas were killed in shark and ray gill nets; seventy-eight were killed during illegal or experimental totoaba fishing; and eleven were killed by trawlers or other gill-netting operations. So it goes.

By 1993, one of the impediments to NAFTA's passage in

Congress was Mexico's lack of environmental standards. Thirty-seven summers after the vaquita was first identified, President Salinas inaugurated the northern part of the Sea of Cortés as a thirty-seven-hundred-square-mile sanctuary in order to protect both the vaquita and the totoaba. Consequently, Salinas decreed, *all* sport and commercial fishing is banned between San Felipe and the Colorado River delta.

Conservationists celebrated. But maps issued to fishermen by PESCA still do not show the biosphere closure, and Deborah and I don't have enough fingers to count all the fishing *pangas* we can see motoring north of San Felipe.

6

Full Reverse

What we eat; what sea lions eat—Honesty of Mexicans—
Puertocitos village—Burnt-out case: the Puertocitos
mechanic—Sea and sky flip

We sleep fitfully under the stars and between our kayaks as scores of inch-long rock roaches (or louses), *Ligia occidentalis,* scurry over us. We could move up higher, but the tickle of roaches, waving antennas in search of algae, is preferable to the snakes or scorpions crawling above.

At dawn a warm wind rifles our bedding; I fire up the stove bleary-eyed. Acidic coffee jolts me awake.

We slip quietly as wavelets into the sea. The orange orb of sun emerges from a square eastern horizon and illuminates everything as it has since the beginning of time, before humans, when the land was a cauldron, when water and ice submerged all. My awe for the cleanness of each morning's sunrise is rooted in privilege: we are witnessing one of the few age-old, natural events unaffected by technology or meddling mankind.

We paddle without stopping, until the sun hangs straight up, then pull into a beach. I slide into the water to cool off and Deborah pulls out the peanut butter. While slugging back the morning's gallon of water, we insert fingers repeatedly into the peanut butter jar, fill our mouths, pass the jar, then slide back down into coolness—the incoming tide is pushing water up from the deep.

Fifty-four pelicans fly overhead in V formation, leading us to the village of Puertocitos. Great blue herons stalk the shoreline with finicky deliberation. Cormorants appear then disappear. Bottlenose dolphins surface and gulp like snorkelers as they suck up to ten quarts of air in a half second. Birds and mammals alike respond to the incoming tide as if a waiter is bearing hors d'oeuvres from the refrigerator.

A sea lion follows Deborah with its whiskered head out of the water, eyes wide and beautiful, an eager flippered canine. Pompano scatter and plop past our bows so the sea lion gives chase. Known to Mexicans as *el lobo* (the wolf), the opportunistic sea lion eats bass, shellfish, anchovies, the toxic scorpion fish, and cusk eels from hundreds of meters below.

While rounding the rocky point a cross surf slams us back and forth, so we slip into spray skirts. Sheer cliffs will prevent us from swimming ashore if we capsize—I feel stupid and helpless that we haven't practiced kayak rescue. I grip my paddle so hard that my hands numb; my right shoulder aches from pulling punches instead of pushing cello strokes. The sea comes from three directions as our bows pop like seafaring jacks-in-the-box. Tomorrow is definitely a rest day.

Before turning a corner into the protected harbor, Isla Lobos glistens white with bird guano. I surf into the still and protected harbor on a last wave, put down the paddle, and shake the numbness out of my hands. Ten yards to starboard, the aquiline snout of a three-foot tortoise surfaces, gurgles like a baby, and plummets.

We set up the tent above high tide line, between two stove-in *pangas,* and go for a walk. We leave seven thousand dollars worth of equipment and expensive kayaks next to Mexican boys wrestling on the sand. While at home, everyone warned us about *bandidos,* mistakenly supposing that border-town behavior would extend to the rural areas we're passing through. Family-oriented Mexican villages do not tolerate criminals and I feel safer here than I would paddling down either coastline of the United States.

In villages more primitive than Puertocitos, bereft of most modern amenities and financial opportunities, the pace of life is dictated by the brutal honesty and simplicities of land and sea. The wind whistles through stark saguaro and sand, as the tide flushes out the harbor and the sun burns down with unmitigated heat; at dawn and dusk here on this edge of desert and sea, on this edge of the world, the light dapples through with a soft clarity that Renoir spent all of his life trying to paint.

In the next month and a half we will walk away from our most important possessions on scores of beaches and even the poorest people will not steal from us because rural Mexican honor is indifferent to the almighty dollar. Three years ago, I left my wallet in a seaside cantina and when the pock-faced, barefoot teenager came running out to return it, he would only accept a "muchas gracias."

Here in Puertocitos, nearly two hundred homes dot the hillsides and half are foreign-owned cottages, circling the harbor and bristling with satellite dishes; Mexican plywood or cinder block homes sprawl on the sandy inland side of Puertocitos like stubborn cacti. Water tanks top hat many of the homes and one form of architecture on the hillsides almost matches the inland dwellings: perched between every home is an outhouse, but the difference between American and Mexican outhouses are the padlocked doors. The first one we come to displays a sign: BANK OF PUERTOCITOS: DEPOSITS ONLY PLEASE.

The town mechanic skids up to us in a yellow dune buggy; Jay is unshaven, smiling, chatty. He points us to the grocery store; he moved here from Alta California nine years ago. "Man, this place is in *full reverse*. And I'm not looking forward to the cold weather—it's coming, I heard about it on TV this morning." He salutes us good-bye with the flatulent squeal of hot rubber on pavement, power shifting into second with a disarming clank of metal against metal—he needs to fix that dune buggy.

Surf crashes over the edge of the hot springs. Spanish explorers described the sulfurous stink, but no early sailor soaked here. We sink back into the ninety-degree, green bath and feel tension bleed out of our knotted backs. As the tide drops lower, and the water gets hotter, we flop down into a lower pool. Frigatebirds ride updrafts above as the tide pulls its fish back down into refrigerator depths.

A balding American expatriate tells us: "Did you know the Japs are paying beaucoup bucks for quote-unquote *research fishing permits?* The mantas and sea cucumbers and billfish all go to Japan. . . . In May of 1992 six squid boats came in and cleaned out all the squid. . . . They cut the fins of sharks and sell 'em as an aphrodisiac." He stubs out his cigarette, looks up, and listens to the surf hitting the breakwater and the wind coming up the harbor. We excuse ourselves in order to batten down our tent, and as we rush off he shouts: "It's already down the tubes and in the next ten years, you watch, it'll be fished out!"

Sleep is impossible as hot gusts lift either end of the tent and drop us. As the wind subsides, sand swirls into our eyelids, fingernails, and ears. Too hot for sheltering in the sleeping bag. Even the rain is warm as I stagger out again and again to restake the tent. If I were a Jesuit missionary stationed here, indoctrinated in the ways of our Lord, there would be only one interpretation about such hot tempests.

In the morning, rumors circulate from the satellite-television viewing locals about a hurricane moving toward the mainland, and more than one Puertocitoan warns us. Suddenly the wind lifts our unattended tent like a kite, bouncing across the beach until it hangs up on a palapa. Three poles are broken. Some Mexican boys help Deborah and me pick up the pieces, scattered across the beach.

Out in the protected harbor, capsizing our sea kayaks takes a concerted effort rather than just an accidental shift of balance. Reboarding by blowing up the "paddle floats" or "sea wings" takes time, so we practice without capsize gear. By simply swimming to the stern, thrusting a leg on either side, and vaulting on top of the boat like Roy Rogers mounting from the rear, we can reboard in seconds. From the swamped cockpit, a few minutes of vigorous thrusting with the bilge pump drains out the water. We capsize repeatedly, partly to understand our boats, mostly to slip our fears.

We depart after dawn; snot-nosed boys wave good-bye on the beach. The low-pressure system can be felt without any barometer, grating against arthritic knees and my surgically reattached shoulder—both results of mountaineering mishaps. This knuckly ache inside me is more than a mood shift or the rasp of old injuries. It would be like the feeling after overeating if our stomachs were several times bigger; it is a pressure like that of the moon moving the tides. If we had more time out here, close to the natural course of events, recording the ebb and flow of own bodies would be more reliable than that of any weather forecast.

Nearing the ghostly Isla Lobos, we pass a trawler at anchor. Several crew members are draped about the deck, sleeping off the previous night's work, oblivious to our passage. A smell of beer and salty blood and paint waters my eyes. The bearded captain snores on his back with his feet propped up against the wheelhouse door; beside the boat a raft of *los lobos* sleep on their backs, flippers to the sky, whiskered noses bobbing like corks.

We pass more trawlers and pelicans—all sleeping. No body stirs.

Without pavement, the coast is deserted and the peace is

as unexpected as a gringo discovering siesta. Up on a flat rock above the water, a sea lion pup basks in the sun with its eyes shut tight. Deborah paddles close and the pup wakes up with a start: identical, open-mouthed surprise stretches across both of their faces.

The old blackened Volcán Prieto rears up into a cinder cone, and thousands of magmaed rocks spill down into the sea. Water hiccups and gurgles up against black boulders that once bubbled and flowed beneath the earth.

Mountains are faded blue-brown and white, the sky pale and washed out, as if the heat has sucked away all that was green and the sun has bleached the land dry. As we round the whirling turquoise waters of Punta Santa Isabel on a current more river than ocean, the silt clears and fish swirl below in a rainbow of kaleidoscopic languor as if the sea and sky have been reversed in some cosmic accident, until we feel closer to flying than floating.

The mechanic was right. This place *is* in full reverse.

7

The Origin of California

The proper name for this peninsula—Rodríguez de Montalvo's work—Hernán Cortés's pursuit of a myth—The legend of Marina

The peninsula we are paddling along is often referred to as "Baja." Although this name has cachet for thousands of boaters, fishermen, and tourists, in Spanish it merely means "lower." Calling it Baja instead of Baja California is like referring to New Mexico as "New."

In the sixteenth century Spaniards began calling this peninsula "California," or "the Californias," and when speaking of the northern region now belonging to the United States, they pronounced it "Alta [Higher] California." The name originated from a sixteenth-century novel, *Las Sergas de Esplandián (The Deeds of Esplandian)*, written by Rodríguez de Montalvo. The author's invention of California might have derived from the Greek words *kalli* and *ornis,* which together mean beautiful bird, referring to the mythical flying carnivores called griffins. It is more likely that Montalvo simply borrowed from the eleventh-century French poem, "Chanson de Roland":

> Dead is my nephew who conquered so many lands!
> And now the Saxons rebel against me
> And the Hungarians, Bulgarians, and many others,
> The Romans, the Puillain, and those of Sicily
> And those of Africa and those of Califerne.

Here "Califerne" refers to the former Muslim rulers of Spain. Before Montalvo even finished *Deeds,* his sequel to the Portuguese novel *Amadís de Gaula,* the imaginations of Europeans were fired by *Amadís*: good Christians everywhere were sailing out into brave new worlds, looking for gold and heathens to convert.

Montalvo had also been influenced by Christopher Columbus's 1492 voyage and his tales of an island en route to the Indies, inhabited only by warlike women. In *Deeds,* Montalvo wrote:

> Know ye that at the right hand of the Indies there is an island named California, very close to that part of the Terrestial Paradise, which was inhabited by black women, without a single man among them, and that they lived in the manner of Amazons. They were robust of body, with strong and passionate hearts and great virtues. The island itself is one of the wildest in the world on account of the bold and craggy rocks. . . . The island everywhere abounds with gold and precious stones, and upon it no other metal was found. They lived in caves well excavated. They had many ships with which they sailed to other coasts to make forays, and the men whom they took as prisoners they killed. . . . In this island, named California, there are many griffins. . . . In no other part of the

world can they be found. . . . [T]here ruled over that island of California a queen of majestic proportions, more beautiful than all others, and in the very vigor of her womanhood.

The queen, Califia, sails to Constantinople with five hundred griffins and all of her Amazon warriors. Joining with the Turks, she wages war against the Christians by releasing the griffins, which attacked allies and foes alike by seizing them, soaring high up into the sky, then dropping them to their deaths. Califia loses the battle, then falls in love with Esplandián. In a manner befitting the time, Califia is converted into a Christian and married to another knight because Esplandián is already betrothed to the emperor's daughter. After the pagan Turks eventually fall to defeat, California and its gold are ceded to the Christians.

Although the California tale does not comprise the entire book, *Deeds* and *Amadís* placed a spin upon developments to come within Mexico or New Spain. The well-read conquistadors were all inspired by these tales of chivalry in foreign lands.

One of Hernán Cortés's soldiers was nick-named after a character in the books. Another companion of Cortés, Bernal Diaz del Castillo, upon encountering one of the towns in Mexico, wrote: "We were amazed, and said it was like the enchantments they tell of in the legend of Amadís." Although these influences of the novels are described by Charles Chapman in his 1928 *A History of California,* Cortés's resurrection of the fictional Esplandián is not mentioned.

During Cortés's first Mexico battle, he slaughtered more than a thousand Tabascan Indians with harquebuses (muskets); the Spaniards suffered two deaths. Cortés was given a Native slave, Marina, as an interpreter. She had an "open-faced," dusky-skinned radiance and promptly became Cortés's mistress; her cultural sensitivities and linguistic savvy probably prevented the Spaniards from being slaughtered. Like Califia (who turned to Christianity), Marina played a vital role in enabling the Christians to conquer the pagan Aztecs, who eventually ceded their gold and their land to the Spanish Christians. Cortés had his first son by Marina, who loved him as devotedly as Califia did Esplandián. After being converted to Christianity she was allowed to marry another soldier, while Cortés later married a daughter of royalty (his second wife).

Cortés now wanted to conquer California, across the sea from New Spain, widely believed to be an island rather than a peninsula. Cortés wrote his fourth letter to King Charles V in 1524:

> . . . there is an island inhabited only by women without any men, and that at given times men from the mainland visit them; if they conceive, they keep the female children to which they give birth, but the males they throw away. This island is ten days journey from the province, and many of them went thither and saw it, and told me also that it is very rich in pearls and gold.

Here, Cortés did not use *California,* even though he had already named the peninsula. Rather than further allude to the fiction that had outlined his conquest of Mexico, it was more important to mention pearls and gold to the king. Without releasing any of the royal treasury, Charles V promised a percentage of future spoils to Cortés, and encouraged him to make further explorations for the Crown.

At first Cortés sent two ships to California. After a mutiny, one ship landed in the Bay of La Paz and began trading trinkets to the Indians for pearls, and abusing the women; the Indian men murdered twenty-one Spaniards. The survivors were later killed by one of Cortés's enemies back on the Mexican mainland.

Cortés was responsible for the slaughter of thousands of men, women, and children; hangings; tortures by mutilation or fire; and probably strangled his first wife. Now Cortés's life took an abrupt turn from the mayhem of mainland Mexico as he attempted to consummate the final part of the myth on "the island" of California.

Cortés first landed on the peninsula and found a few legendary pearls, but no gold, while the primitive Indian women and their jealous husbands did not match the glorious Montalvo myths of Califia and the menless Amazons. Cortés retreated to the mainland to fetch more food, and upon his return, he experienced another California legend. The men he had left behind were dying of starvation and circling high in the air above there would have been turkey vultures (griffins), sensing death from miles away and biding their time as twenty-three of his soldiers died in abject hunger, ignorant to the sea's food that could have saved them, and deaf to the prayers of Cortés. He abandoned California.

Cortés sent more ships across the sea, but no one found any gold. For another 150 years, maps continued to show California as an island. Since Cortés had many detractors his namesake sea was often called Vermilion (*Bermejo*). In the early twentieth century, the newly independent Mexican government renamed it the Gulf of California, trying to erase all connections with their conquistador heritage.

The expeditions cost Cortés 300,000 *castellanos* of gold, or 600,000 silver pesos, a small fortune even for a successful sixteenth-century conqueror. Combined with the excesses of his estate in Oaxaca, Cortés claims that he plunged into debt. He spent the last seven years of his life in Spain, showering lawsuits upon the diffident royal court. He died at sixty-three years old in 1547.

Marina earned a type of eternity. Mexican schoolchildren recite her legend as aptly as Americans tell of Paul Revere; Marina was an Indian slave who influenced the outcome of Mexican history and married into wealth; and she did not marry Cortés. Mexico also celebrates Columbus Day (who never landed on the Mexican mainland). Celebrating Cortés would be anathema to Mexico.

8

Huerfanito y Bahía Gonzaga

A hard-drinking retiree of Huerfanito—Renaming the sea—
Frigatebirds robbing boobies—A yellow-bellied sea snake—
Slack-bellied, venomous Americans

In six hours we paddle seventeen miles. Miles and hours are important in case of emergencies, in case we have to get somewhere fast. But we have another place for miles and hours: we put them into our journals as brief notes and they get buried by a sea of sights, sounds, texture, and smells that enrich our days.

The hamlet of Huerfanito (the orphan) has sixteen houses and a landing strip behind the beach. It's a retirement community, and even though we're curious, we want to avoid partying Americans. After dithering out in the surf, reluctant to get caught out in a growing wind, we surf into the northern end of the beach and cook bean burritos.

A septuagenarian pulls up on a three wheeler, says some-

thing; we cup hands to our ears; he twists a key, shutting off the growling engine, and says it again: "C'mon over for a beer." Like most Americans we meet, Pete is concerned. "You're paddling *all* the way down Baja?"

"Yes," I reply, "as far as we can down the peninsula."

He warns us about venturi winds and although we listen politely, it is typical to be inundated with expert advice because adventurers are considered inexpert fools by locals.

Pete tells about a sixteen-foot boat capsizing off Isla Muerto in the winds a couple of weeks ago. Three of the fishermen swam to shore, but a man and his twelve-year-old son never made it. Several days later they were found floating fifteen miles south, the son without a head and the father missing most of his chest. "Sharks," Pete says, catching our eyes then looking out to our little boats, shaking his head.

"And you know that that island Muerto, means 'dead' in Spanish?" We nod about the Mexican preoccupation with death. Because of the abundance of Dead Bays, Dead Points, Dead Islands, and Dead Beaches on our map, I have crossed out "Sea of Cortés" and scrawled in "the Dead Sea."

Pete complains that he is always the one to get sent out on rescue missions, since "I'm the only pilot around here"—not mentioning the community of fifty gringo pilots just south of here. Pete then abruptly asks if we met Jay in Puertocitos.

"The guy that tears around in a yellow dune buggy?" I ask.

"That *jackass*," Pete roars, "he's supposed to be fixing my transmission, not driving it!"

The pitch of wind increases and we hustle to Pete's driveway: his airplane is hopping up and down so he leans against the ropes to cinch down the wings. Inside his ranch-style home, he pops open Coronas and warns us that Mexican fishermen are thieves and we should never turn our backs. Although his ranting is more about fishermen than race, more crotchety cynicism than cultural bias, I object: "The fishermen we met three years ago are some of the kindest people on earth."

When Pete runs out of steam he turns on the television and surfs repeatedly through the channels—he has nearly fifty—reaching down from his recliner to open the cooler and another fizzing Corona. We excuse ourselves.

A wind generator howls. Orion sparkles above. And the sea licks the sterns of our boats; Deborah ties them to an old rusted boat anchor so they won't blow away.

A ribby Mexican dog, Sultan, slinks sideways to our tent for handouts, all ready to run in case we should beat him. In most of Mexico, dogs don't get fed; so dogs steal food. Consequently, dogs get beaten. Mexican dogs that aren't already road pizza are bruised, scabby, desultory, and insecure; if they get sick, they die. As Deborah coaxes Sultan to accept a pat, she asks if the inhumanity extended toward most dogs here is the same pattern shown to the creatures of the sea.

"If we were poor, wouldn't we beat the dogs?" I reply.

Deborah shoots me that silent, taking-my-temperature look, crossing her dark eyebrows as if to say, *Since when did you become a bleeding heart?*

Once we round an arm south of Huerfanito, it's blowing so hard that we're being shoved out to sea, out to Isla Muerto. We've heard enough to avoid visiting this island—profiling a dead man's head and body—so I scream for the nonplussed Deborah to paddle in. Tendons click in my arms as I pull against wind and sea. I swallow a wave; salt rims my nose and lips. It takes half an hour to paddle a hundred yards into a sheltered sand cove.

Big fish are driving little smelts up to the shore as thick as silver pellets of rain and they wriggle and die by the thousands while two yellow-footed gulls stand by disinterested. Legions of pelicans between here and Isla Muerto are dive-bombing or swimming with their mouths open, ducking their heads for ten seconds to let the water drain out, then repeating the process, all the while harassed by gulls. No bird works hard to eat.

I cast in a lure and within seconds I am attached to a ten-pound fighter, almost too much fish for the tiny rod. Catch enough fish and the line becomes an inverse umbilical cord: cut it loose and you give the fish its life; reel it in and you will kill it. The fish is crazed from gorging on smelts and after flipping my rod tip inland just once, it rushes the shore like a suicidal whale. At my feet the croaker "croaks" audibly—so I breathe deep and turn away from Deborah to run the blade through its spinal cord. As it croaks, burps, and gulps one last time beneath my bloody hand, as if by signal, two western gulls come squawking in. I cut the croaker up, fling the innards to the sea, and the gulls chase them out, squabbling madly.

The meat is slightly brown and parts between our teeth like trout. At "Baja Midnight" (9 P.M.) we retire to our bed of sand beneath a protected bluff. The sea is muted and we sip chamomile tea as the wind swirls beneath a crescent moon. Thick calluses on my palms click against the cup; the last honey-eyed sip is mixed with grit.

We clip our boats side by side with carabiners. We unstrap our mast riggings from the deck shock cords, hoist up our two sails, and the wind snaps against nylon and pushes us south in sudden acceleration. As soon as our speed matches the wind, we no longer feel it pushing our hair. The tight ache in our arms and shoulders makes the north wind an unexpected gift.

Three long-billed curlews labor against the wind. Brown boobies swing out of their horizontal flights into straight vertical plunges, flapping to speed their descent, tucking their wings at the last instant, and knifing into the water. The early Spaniards named them *bobos,* or "stupid fellows," because the nesting boobies made no attempt to escape from hungry sailors.

The wind stops. As we trim our sails, a yellow-bellied sea snake swims in circles. Its neurotoxin—more powerful than that of rattlesnakes, cobras, or coral snakes—could paralyze

both of us, so we keep our hands high on the paddles, away
from its tiny teeth. No bird or fish preys upon it, and we specu-
late that some sort of chemical emission or its splashy, bright
yellow spots serve as a warning sign. If we should see many
more of these paddle-tailed beauties, snorkeling might become
too nerve-racking.

In Gonzaga Bay, we beach onto a long sand spit at noon.
Thirty small planes sit beside seventy-one beach cottages, inhabited by one permanent gringo resident. At a Mexican cinder
block house and restaurant, Alphonsina's, three Americans fill
our water containers and offer us beer.

Barney, a garrulous aficionado of all things Baja California,
is "the mayor of the spit." He points to a distant crane on one
of the many stretches of white-sand shoreline; a turd-brown
water-tank tower of a desalination plant sits further north. Barney winkingly refers to the Mexican businessmen building con-
dos as "tomato growers" (squinting his eyes and pretending to
toke off a joint); all the American regulars here are whining
about these new developments inside "their" bay. Dishes clat-
ter, Barney's San Diego investor friend burps, and a Cessna 180
buzzes noisily down the strip, its pilot escaping the coming tide
in order to rejoin the Monday morning parade into Los Angeles, U.S.A.

Last spring, two trawlers pulled into Gonzaga Bay for an
evening's vacuuming, turning the waters bright with fish-draw-
ing halogen lights. By noon the trawlers were gone. The spit
residents found thirty-five dolphins washed up on the bay
shores, all with .22-caliber bullet holes in their heads. "It ain't
the first time that's happened here either," Barney says.

The investor tells us about the Hispanic immigration into
Alta California. He is my age, with blow-dried hair, wearing a
perfect sunlamp tan, a polo shirt, and leather thongs. We are
half naked, pasted with sand and white salt brine, unshaven
and barefoot; now I can guess what it must have been like for
indigenous Californians to meet conquistadors. "These goddamned beaners," he nods toward Alphonsina's daughter, "have

destroyed our economy and you watch," he says, too loudly for
comfort. "California is a paradigm for the rest of our country.
The beaners are eventually gonna destroy everything." The ex-
pression is new to me, so when I ask for its meaning, he
replies, "It's all beaners eat, man: beans."

Deborah stares into her ice tea; I watch the investor. Of
course, the peninsula draws all types: burnt-out drug cases
who disappear into the loosely structured Mexican society;
folks car-camping on beaches half the year; sport fishermen
(rarely women); and men like the investor in front of us, ex-
hibiting propriety airs in a foreign country. Ugly Americans pre-
dominate here, partly because they are loud, and in a country
as economically depressed as Mexico, money imbues the up-
per-middle-class Alta Californian with an irresistible sense of
power.

When an American teenager starts yelling about the tee
shirt size he wants to purchase, "Extra large, extra large, extra
large," to Alphonsina's young daughter—as if she were deaf instead of unable to speak English, which is considered a simple
and unromantic language by most Mexicans—it is time to go.

9

If You Build It, They Will Come

Stricken by the sunset—First sailor—Japanese and a Hollywood director go fishing—How to kill fish; how to eat fish; how to say grace

The western sky is crimson as our hulls scrape up against a white Bahía Gonzaga beach. The eastern sky cloaks us in darkness. We stand agape. I have never seen the sky bleed with such magnificence—it has something to do with the sunset reflection from the distant Pacific refracting under a ceiling of storm clouds. Maybe it has been too long since I have watched sunsets. Is it true that we watch sunsets when we are young, but as we grow busier and older, we don't have time, or more precisely, *make* time to appreciate the sky's pastels?

We have beached next to a sign—too dark to see. I take

out my headlamp and read it aloud: NO CAMPING HERE. We laugh riotously. The sign is in English, so the dozen houses beyond and the people therein who erected the sign must be Americans. We lay out pads and sleeping bag.

Punta Final is rough but manageable. The sea greets the rocky point as an old adversary, punching the bottom then reaching sixty feet up the weathered cliff face with a white-handed, vaporous slap. We give it a half-mile berth.

In September of 1539, Francisco de Ulloa, under the orders of Hernán Cortés, was the first white man to sail these waters. He rounded Punta Final and wondered what lay ahead.

There are no roads or camps, only powerful currents and inaccessible mountains. The entire horizon is a cliffed shoreline fighting the chopped sea. The water stretches as an ebony infinity, moving underneath us like a great inviolate animal and mirroring the sky. We are far enough out that the *campos* behind have disappeared and the shore stretches as the same beach that Ulloa saw four centuries ago, a beach that yawns past our own short lives as if mere grains of sand.

My pulse races. I steal a quick glance sideways to my partner: she's smiling. Between the crashing surf and the musky sea and the unknowns of our commitment ahead I have not felt so alive in years.

Bahía Gonzaga is one of the most pristine of all white-sand beaches in the Americas. If it were in a different country, or more accessible, it would be groomed like Hilton Head, Acapulco, or Rio de Janeiro. Although the abrasive sands of progress have arrived in the form of American money brokers and Mexican marijuana growers, Bahía Gonzaga is still hard to reach. The dirt road is rent by washboards. Private planes only fit a few people. And there are no five-star hotels.

Development might come slow, but it will come. As inexorably as building a baseball diamond in the middle of somecornfieldnowhere, the heavy hitters will come. One could only hope that they consult the past before destroying the future.

I turn to look back, my neck popping painfully, taking a last glance at Bahía Gonzaga. In 1539, Ulloa described it:

> I found it to be a port as fine as big as could be. Once inside, it is so closed in on all sides that the sea is not visible. The bottom is clean and of any depth those who enter it wish to seek. It has two large clean entrances, free of obstacles, formed by the island. Inside we found so many seals that were I to say there were a hundred thousand I think I would not be exaggerating. For this reason we named it "El Puerto de los Lobos."

These sixteenth-century sailors accepted their own bountiful Mediterranean Sea beneath Spain as status quo. For them to comment upon an even greater abundance shows why the Sea of Cortés is the richest body of water on the planet. In 1602, during a voyage similar to Ulloa's, Father Antonio de la Acensión described "a great quantity of fish of many species and different forms . . ." that tasted "good" and included pilchards, sole, newts, porpoises, hammerhead sharks, stingrays, manta rays, bonitos, muttonfish, roncadors, mackerel, oysters, salmon, tuna, sardines, red snapper, dogfish, and more sharks.

Journey of the Flame is a fanciful biography that conveys a nineteenth-century Mexican's perspective of the sea. Nothing changed for two hundred years. The subject, Don Juan Obrigón, speaks of "vast quantities of animal life . . . Whales crowded the bays so that it seemed possible to step from one to the other for miles." As the leviathans rose, multitudes of fish and birds fell off the great backs.

By 1940 something was changing, but its impact wouldn't be noticed for fifty years. John Steinbeck spent two months collecting biological specimens from a fishing boat. In his book, *Log from the Sea of Cortez,* he described twelve Japanese shrimp trawlers working the sea, systematically pulling up and killing every living creature. He concluded that "they were committing a true crime against nature and against the immediate welfare of Mexico and the eventual welfare of the whole human species."

Commercial fishing has wreaked the greatest havoc upon the sea. Although the impact of sportfishing doesn't compare with commercial fishing, lack of respect for the resource is the common denominator. In 1967 a book of fishing stories, *The Sea of Cortez,* introduced the waters to modern sportfishermen. The author, Ray Cannon, describes "fish pileups": starting with a small area of motionless water beginning to stir, Cannon describes how the sea eventually transforms into mile-wide boils. "All carnivores become as if insane," he wrote, "and they gorge, disgorge, and gorge again. Maddened by the blood and by greed, they slash and rip and kill even their own kind." Cannon sketches creatures "with mouths large enough to gulp in a beer keg" rising from two hundred feet below; men ducking as a dolphin leaps over their heads; and a pelican kamikaze-diving into their speeding boat.

Although this former Hollywood director liked to stretch a good yarn, *The Sea of Cortez* had the effect of a reckless work of nonfiction. In the mind of any reader who wanted to fish— by yarding up totoaba, snook, golden grouper, and every other fish of the sea, then sharing his unerring technique—Cannon introduced a myth to thousands of fishermen. It was a myth more farcical than Montalvo's sixteenth-century tale luring the conquistadors to gold and Amazon women. Cannon's book was reprinted several times and baited three generations of fishermen to believe that the Sea of Cortés was a limitless horn-of-plenty.

We stop, frightened by the waves, at a break in the cliffs. I paddle in first, holding my breath until the fiberglass hull scrapes barnacled boulders; I jump out and breathe again, waving Deborah in.

As Deborah washes our clothes in the surf, I walk the

boulders to sheltered fishing. On my second cast, the spoon plops behind a wave and settles briefly, until dinner tugs back. On the next wave, I bring it in: a several pound spotted sand bass. As I saw out its guts, a turkey vulture beats past then circles lazily above. Two yellow-footed gulls fight for the intestines.

Keeping and eating your own fish in this day of catch and release would make you feel old-fashioned and even exploitative *if* you killed more than you could eat. But I have never understood fishing for sport. Since I was ten years old, bait fishing with bacon and hot dogs in Florida canals, my aim was bringing home food. Sitting on the canal walls and staring into the waters for hours on end also brought home a sense of connection with the natural world, a closeness that was otherwise blocked by growing up in the cement jungles of modern urbania.

As a youth, another important lesson about fishing involved the origin of food. Rather than emanating beneath cellophane and on top of foam at the grocery store, food I learned, was a living, breathing organism not altogether different from me. I would not have understood this if I didn't *experience* the connection while fishing.

If the fish was safe to eat, I killed it immediately. Otherwise, I removed the hook and released the fish in the water. I let stingrays go by cutting the line. Part of the allure, I admit, was a curiosity about the mysterious presents of the sea: every time something from the deep pulled on my "umbilical cord," it became an opportunity to open up a new gift—or to return it to the protective womb of water. My family celebrated each catch because fish were no longer plentiful in the canals and because it was one of life's privileges to catch and eat your own fish.

I think about those Florida canals as I carry the bass to camp. No doubt our own ancestors once crawled out of the sea looking more lurid than the bass that is still warm against my palm; I am naked and shivering. The vulture watches from above.

I am here to repeat my childhood rituals and feel connected to this sea, the greatest exemplar of protozoic, gelatinous, and spiny life-forms left on the planet. The oft-held
theory (or excuse) put forth by hunters of needing to kill in order to identify with our caveman hunting instincts seems
ephemeral and fatuous next to identifying with the animal itself. But trying to become closer to an animal by killing it is
merely mistakenly identified blood lust, or playing God.

I do not fear reincarnation so much as the knowledge that
the fish and I are related, if only by virtue of sharing the same
planet. So every time I sever a fish's spinal column I can imagine my own death. And surely I will follow this bass at my own
journey's end. If there is any lesson here, it is to kill as few fish
as possible because the bass I clutch is the progenitor of my
own original aqueous form.

No amount of sugar in the Earl Gray tea will offset the
briny well water I filled up on several days south. Deborah
fixes rice while I panfry the bass with an onion over a small
driftwood fire. Oil spits out of the pan and I turn my face. I say
"thank you" for the bass, and instead of directing my apprecia-
tion to the heavens, I look to the sea from whence our original
form crawled so many millennia ago.

10

Robbing the Godless

*Francisco de Ulloa first meets the Californians—Six
harquebuses are fired—Molesting Indian women—Story of
a pearl*

We pass the deep canyon arroyos and impenetrable mountains
of the Calamajue region. In 1766, the Calamajue Mission lasted
only a year before the Jesuit father moved to greener pastures
and friendlier Indians. The only twentieth-century inroad on
this stretch is the isolated fishcamp of Campo Calamajue. The
pescadores (fishermen) act indifferent, even though sea kayakers rarely pass. In the early light, their hair is combed, their
faces are clean-shaven, and the fishing nets are stacked with
the fastidiousness one gives to a parachute before jumping
from an airplane. Some of the men have the broad lips and
aquiline noses of mainland Indian blood; most are mestizo—
Spanish mixed with Indian, with a *café con pocito leche* skin,
and dark brooding eyes. The two men in their *panga* pore over

their net like crocheters, holding their heads high, their backs ramrod straight. The original Baja Californian blood is long gone, and even the mixed blood of these two proud men is without roots on the peninsula; they are replacing a culture wiped off the earth.

Sixteenth-century Spaniards treated the indigenous Californians brutally. During an early Cortés expedition to Santa Cruz (La Paz), soldiers were killed by the Pericú for raping their women; in retribution, an unknown number of Californians died. Ulloa tried to capture some Indians during the third Cortés-financed expedition, but was unable to do so, "inasmuch as they had suffered the first time [Cortés] came there, they retired into safety inland so that we could not get a man out of them."

Although these Christian soldiers must have been fascinated about pagan cultural encounters, the Christian view ultimately reflected contempt and disdain. They wanted pearls and gold. Due to their initial treatment, the Californians shunned soldiers as well as missionaries.

Outside of Bahía Gonzaga, on October 3, 1539, Ulloa wrote about a Californian tribe never contacted by Europeans:

> . . . [W]e saw on shore an old man and another young man with three or four boys. Seeing us approaching them, the young man demanded of one of the boys his bows and arrows which he had left at a little distance. When the boy had fetched them, he took the bow and tried it, apparently to see if it were strung. He and the rest stood still where they were, without any harm or fear, although we were coming close to them. Seeing them so assured we thought they must not be alone but rather had some ambuscade laid, and that their assurance was a ruse.

Ulloa landed in the protection of a gully so that he would not be ambushed and then "seized" the old man, who covered his eyes, as if seeing Spaniards was staring into the sun. They could make no sense of his language, despite Ulloa's interpreters, whom Cortés had seized from La Paz. Ulloa noted their unroofed, grass enclosure next to the sea, some fish, but no bread (which the Spaniards craved), sea lion water pouches, and cane rafts—with "two small badly made paddles" for fishing. Judging these people to be "nomads, possessed of little intelligence," Ulloa released them.

The people of midpeninsula—the Cochimi and the Guaycura—were hunters and gatherers. Although tribes living around the Colorado River delta practiced agriculture, the barren peninsula to the south insulated the Cochimi and the Guaycura in the stone age.

Ulloa discovered that the Cochimi were more adept in the water than the Spanish sailors—despite his observations about their primitive gear. While further south of Bahía Gonzaga, he postponed sailing when some natives paddled out to his frigate. Like most early Spanish narratives, in his Ulloa does not describe his primary purpose: to find pearls or gold. But he could not entice the natives to come close enough to the ship to barter. His narrative continues:

> I went out after them in a boat to see if I could take some one of them so as to give him things and release them. I overtook the one who seemed to be of more importance than the others, for he was the one who came nearest and talked the most—the one who had come out first on the first raft—and when we came up with him he left his raft and dived into the sea and swam. I kept after him for more than half an hour but could not capture him, for every time the boat reached him he dived under the bow and after quite a while came up beyond the stern. Although we exerted ourselves to turn the boat quickly and go after him again, he had meanwhile rested, floating on the water, in order to do the same thing again; and so he

kept it up with good spirit and without weakening in the least until he had so tired us out that those who rowed the boat could no longer start it going. His companions came to his assistance on the other rafts, and seeing that we could not take him I returned to the ships.

Ulloa described these men as naked and handsome, their hair trimmed two or three fingers long. He doesn't mention pearls, but inferring that nothing is to be gained from the Indians, he continues his voyage around the peninsula and up the Pacific Ocean, "punishing" and killing more recalcitrant natives "of wretched habits" by firing upon them with the cannon, loosing dogs, or shooting them with harquebuses. Ulloa continued north toward Alta California, seeking riches for the Crown, but due to mutiny or accident, he and his ship separated from the flotilla and never returned.

Others sought pearls. The next written record of a California expedition was in 1564. Baltasar Obregón wrote, "It is an island of thorny thickets and inhabited by naked cannibals, the most uncivilized, immodest, dirty and vile which have yet been seen or discovered in the Indies." Obregón lauded their ability to dive for oysters. Even though the natives had irreparably charred their pearls by opening the oysters in fires, Obregón felt that future expeditions could obtain large quantities of pearls. He recommended that the king attempt colonization in order to acquire slaves and plant the faith of the Lord. In the style of the day, Obregón couldn't resist further propagating the old California myth: "It is believed that the coast and mainland are inhabited by many people, and it is possible that they wear clothes and possess silver and gold."

A decade later, King Philip II attempted to regulate Spanish discoveries by issuing licenses. According to the terms of the license, settlers could not injure the natives, and settlers had to try and convert these heathens into Christians. In 1593, under the directions of the king, Sebastián Vizcaíno was given a license by the viceroy of New Spain, even though there was some doubt about Vizcaíno's ability to prevent soldiers from committing further "outrages on the natives." Three years later, the viceroy assigned a large number of soldiers, wives, Cristóbal López (a page courting the viceroy's sister), and three Franciscans to fulfill the king's demands about conversions.

Once in California, Vizcaíno wrote that the natives were:

> so bestial and uncivilized, that whether standing or seated, whenever they take the notion, they attend to the necessities of nature without any nicety or respect. Their language is so barbarous that it sounds more like the bleating of sheep than the speech of men.

Vizcaíno left his seven-year-old son, the friars, some soldiers, and all of the wives in Santa Cruz where Cortés had abandoned his settlement. He renamed it La Paz (Peace), after the friendly disposition of the Indians—despite Cortés's previous abuses. The friars (whom Cortés did not bring) were largely responsible for this peace. On October 3, 1596, Vizcaino continued north in two smaller ships to look for pearls and food.

Ten days later, he sailed to Bahía Concepción and encountered several Indians in canoes. Because they seemed more "warlike and daring" than the La Paz natives, he rowed ashore with fifty armed men and let the Indians escort him a mile and a quarter inland to a lake of sweet water. Vizcaíno wrote:

> From there we went on with them to their settlements where they gave us another small good bit of fish, all with much joy, but, it appearing to me that they were much too forward and being suspicious of them, I ordered my men to return slowly toward the beach in the order in which we had come.

Not wanting to anger the king, Vizcaíno omitted the following events from his narrative—while another sailor, Gonzalo de Francia, confessed in a different narrative. Apparently, the viceroy's man, Cristóbal López, had joined Vizcaíno's expedition because he needed a pearl. His fiancée, Doña Elvira (sister of the viceroy), told López she would only consent to marriage if López replaced a magnificent pearl she had lost.

According to Francia, when López saw a California woman with a beautiful pearl hanging from her lip, he snatched it and smashed her with the butt of his harquebus. Two Indians were killed. Vizcaíno's narrative omits the theft and murders:

> As we were marching on, when we had arrived near it [the beach], we saw some arrows fall in the midst of the squadron, and turning about we saw up to a hundred Indians coming behind us shooting arrows at us. I ordered a halt and a face about, and caused four harquebuses to be fired over them to frighten them. Although they were terrorized by the noise when they saw that our weapons did no damage they soon began again to shoot arrows at us with greater violence. I then ordered six harquebuses to be fired, the weapons being lowered, and this time three fell dead on the ground and others, I know not how many, were wounded. At this all fled together and we came on little by little to the shallop [rowboat] of our ship.

While Vizcaíno argued with his soldiers about killing more of their enemy, hundreds of natives gathered. Twenty-five Spaniards who had remained on shore quickly jumped into the second shallop and started rowing back to the ship. As arrows rained down upon the Spaniards, they ducked and dodged to one side, capsizing the shallop. Eighteen soldiers drowned because of their heavy leather armor, while seven men, all wounded, managed to swim back to the ship. Vizcaíno retreated to La Paz.

The Franciscans had built a small church. According to one of the friars, the Indians were fond of the men of the cloth, but disliked the men of armor and deerskins who regularly ripped possessions off the Indians' bodies and molested women—of whom the Indian men were possessive. In his narrative to the king, Vizcaíno declared that there was not enough food to sustain his people, and after a fire swept through their huts, the colony was abandoned for New Spain.

The viceroy later reprimanded Vizcaíno for not punishing Cristóbal López for the incident with the natives. And after López married the viceroy's sister and presented her with the pearl stolen from the Indian, the bride confessed that she had never really lost her pearl.

11

October 12 and 13

*Looking for news in the sky—A near miss sailing—What fear
feels like—Attacking dog and a pack of sea lions—
Delphinoid dreaming*

As night lifts, the sky is clear—except for a puffball cloud
doffed over Isla Angel de la Guarda like an undersized fedora.
From traveling in tempestuous regions I have the unrelenting
habit of studying the sky to assess whether or not it will storm.

Once, halfway up Denali, we radioed out for a weather re-
port: my ranger partners forecasted the worst storm of the
summer, due at sunrise. We abandoned our summit attempt
and spread the news around camp. Climbers spent the afternoon digging bombproof caves, igloos, and ice walls. The next
day dawned clear; I have seldom trusted a radio or a forecast
since. Now I have the unrelenting habit of studying the sky and
forsaking radios.

Rings around the sun or the moon indicate moisture in the

upper atmosphere. Mare's tails or flying-saucer-shaped clouds mean high winds and a change of weather. Aching joints equal low pressure systems, usually followed by wind or rain. Red dawns mean trouble. Mornings of cold, still, crystalline air—making the sort of cobalt sky, calm sea, and clear liquid sunrise of this particular dawn—are traveling days.

Most of Baja California is desert. It's the sort of place where you can get away with sleeping directly under the stars, like the original Californians did. This saves us the chore of pitching and unpitching the tent, and allows fraternization with passing roaches, crabs, and reptiles. I always thump out my water shoes before each morning's donning.

My $12.99 watch says it's Tuesday October 12, 6:30 A.M., which means nothing out here. Like most mornings, I shake Deborah awake. She hates early starts, even though the afternoon winds are dangerous. Back at Punta Final we entered a region inhabited mostly by the sea. Here, coyotes are rumored to flick fat, ruddy tails into the sea to catch dinner, switching the tail back when crabs latch on. Even the fishermen concede this desolate, roadless section of coast to the coyotes and their wild, rabid, and furry neighbors.

We unload several hundred pounds of gear, carry the boats ninety yards down green-greased and gray-barnacled boulders, and set the boats just above the waterline. We carry down all of the gear and reload.

Loading a kayak takes some science. We squeeze the heavy items—water, stove, fuel, tent, books, and food—into the front hatch to give our bows authority in big seas. In the rear hatch, to offset our body weight on the stern, we stuff the lighter sleeping bag, pads, and clothing. The rubber-gasketed hatches seal tight and waterproof, but just for insurance we cram all of our gear into coated nylon "dry bags." After an hour of packing, we're off.

A dearth of birds suggests that the fish are gone. Six pelicans fly north, so high that only a trawler-sized whale shark could divert their attention. The wind comes and I holster my paddle.

By the time I have unraveled and hauled my sail, Deborah has paddled a half mile south. At first, sailing at an effortless, four- to five-mile-per-hour pace is exhilarating. I catch Deborah in half an hour. The wind gusts so hard that I must lean into it to prevent capsizing. Between working the rudder, holding the sheet, leaning for balance, and watching for big waves, getting scared would ruin my concentration. If my anxiety levels could be charted, there is a point when the curve—or my blood pressure—climbs beyond mere exhilaration and too many things start happening simultaneously; only a fool would miss the cue of a heart beating out of control. Now I am right on the edge, one more element to cope with and my chart climbs into high blood pressure, into that adrenaline-filled territory of increasing terror.

Getting around Punta Bluff will require more of an easterly course, even though the wind is blowing due south. Although I can't sail upwind without more sail and a keel board, I tack with my rudder and slip closer to the surf-ravaged cliffs of Punta Bluff. Momentarily, I am going to have to stop sailing and paddle furiously if I want to clear Punta Bluff, and while trying to decide when, the wind gusts: ripping the sheet from my hand, torquing the boat sideways until only the energy of the epoxied mast breaking loose from between my feet prevents a capsize. The mast sags dangerously starboard, so I lean to port and my throat expands, with a sensation akin to drinking too much coffee; my heart must be visibly palpating against my paddle jacket. My blood pressure shoots up into fear: I could lose it.

Deborah immediately comes to my rescue, steadying my boat and handing me the sail so I can reef it down. It is foolish to be sailing in these conditions, but she says nothing and I love her for that.

The seven-foot mast is lurching back and forth like a pole in a tetherball tournament. I can't dissemble it without landing, and the shore is cliffed. We're soaked with spray, my cramped feet can't feel the rudder pedals, and the waters east of the point are the only thing I've seen yet that resemble a legendary "fish pileup."

We paddle east, putting our shoulders into and concentrating on each paddle stroke in order to clear the cliffs; surf slamming and roaring gives us incentive and paddling power never previously realized. A half mile out, we push rudder pedals south, allowing us to see the northbound tide colliding with the southbound wind. Big trouble. We're already committed and the wind is blowing too strong for us to turn around, so we hold our breaths and plunge in. Our boats are slammed back and forth until forward movement becomes the only promise of stability, but each time we are punched in one direction, we brace our paddles on the other side—compromising forward movement. As we round the point, a sleeping colony of sea lions awakens and fifty anxious females charge en masse, barking in our ears like a pack of hungry jackals and breaking our concentration. Although the frothing water doesn't deter sea lions, if they bump and capsize us, it would be difficult to keep our heads above the waves. And even if we could swim in this conundrum of sea lions, tide, wind, and water, the violence of sea slamming the cliffed shore would prevent us from getting out. Resenting my helplessness, and harnessing every neuron in my lungs, I shout back at *los lobos:* "Shutthehellup!" which seems to increase their ruckus—*OW-OW-OW-OW-OW-OW-OW*—until it matches that of the sea. Shouting and losing it for a bit is like a good slap in the face, like admitting to myself *you don't need to panic Jon-boy.*

It is at these times—judging from other experiences—when retreat is cut off and the proverbial guard dogs lick their chops, that you can rise somewhere above calamity and find a place of inner calm and strength. A place outside of yourself where you can see your actions as an objective observer and you stop being scared; you stop yelling. You stop thinking about what to do and begin performing by instinct alone. Time slows to a crawl and instead of pumping out, your blood pressure drops and you go on automatic pilot and lose yourself.

One day working at the American Guard Dog Agency in Phoenix and passing by the kennels all fifty-two dogs lunge toward me and hit the cage doors with their jaws clacking and foaming madly. When I approach the big white shepherd out in the yard so that he can try and rip my arms off, I slip and fall beneath his legs—the same shepherd who put my predecessor in the hospital—I am too cocky to be wearing the protective vest or helmet and I am supine on the dewy grass as time slows to a crawl and White Fang darts for my throat: I thrust out the padded burlap sleeve and he mistakes it for my arm like he is supposed to and begins shredding the burlap until I have a precious second to roll out of his thirty-foot leash range. When I am clear, he lunges and pulls with such fury that the main miracle seems to be that the leash doesn't break. I quit my job right there.

By the time I consider throwing *los lobos* a doggie bone, I am giggling with adrenaline. Punta Bluff is behind us, Deborah is cursing with relief, my hands are tingling pins and needles, and my cramped feet are pulsing like abscessed teeth. I pull into a sheltered cove of scuttling sally lightfoot crabs and reach skyward to dissemble my swaying mast.

Northern Baja California is not shredded by commercial jets, let alone small planes. It is human nature only to miss something when it's gone. To wit: if we had been hearing jets for the last week, we wouldn't have thought to complain. Most of the wildest refuges on the planet—the Arctic, Denali National Park, even the Himalaya—have their ceilings regularly torn and violated by jet aircraft. Not here. I tell Deborah; she grins.

"And you know Deb," I add, "we haven't seen people or boats for two days."

I howl toward the sea as a Cochimi might have. My clothes and hair are starched with salt; I spit sand out of my mouth. I am so dehydrated that my bowels haven't moved in three days.

Deborah's neck is so sore that she hasn't been able to look behind without turning her whole boat, so I knead her neck slowly, drawing figure eights with my fingers over the bony clavicular knob, elastic muscled skin, and the three-inch rubbery sun cancer scar—the surgeon diagnosed it benign, but her father's death from melanoma is a constant reminder of the downside of adventuring under the sun.

I lay my leaking, inflatable sleeping pad out on the rocks and prepare our bed. Deborah reads aloud from the beginning of a novel about mountain men and buffalo disappearing from the West.

I wake up five seconds before my 6:30 watch alarm sounds. It reads "Wednesday October 13"; who cares? I silence the alarm and let Deborah sleep as I study the clear sky. To my amazement, the puffball cloud still caps Isla Ángel de la Guarda.

The sea is at a curious apogee, a slack tide that renders this rounded world flat. Forty yards out, the sea splashes. Three darkened bottlenose dolphins are rippling along as clean and quiet as knives, herding small fish, splashing out of the water and into our bay. *Are they sending us food?*

I shake Deborah awake, but she will not look seaward where I am silently pointing. She confronts me instead, and I imagine her as our unborn daughter, frustration firing the pupils behind her sleep-swollen eyelids. She is mad because I have stolen her from a dream with three dolphins trying to talk to us with high frequency whistles; Deborah is frustrated because in the dream we couldn't understand them. By the time I get her to look to the sea they have vanished.

12

The Heathens

Stars, moon, and sun diving into the sea—Christian conversions—The first settlement—Recycling pitaya fruit— Violent Spaniards

While lying in dawn, I can imagine the former Californians. These people bivouacked inside stone walls, curled up with spouses and children to stay warm, and watched the sky. I imagine their version of gods while studying the sky.

The Guaycura tribe believed that the stars, the moon, and the sun were men and women who dove out of sight every twelve hours and reemerged on the other side of the day by swimming. The Cochimi tribe believed that the Great Captain had made the sky and all of the earth. His adopted child, Emai Cuano, sweetened bitter seeds, tamed the animals, and created fire under the earth to keep humans warm. When the humans complained of the heat, Emai Cuano pulled away the upper layer of soil and created the sea with his saliva. When men tried to get rid of the water, Emai Cuano created rain with his tears.

The men and women fashioned mother-of-pearl oyster shells strung like beads around their necks, while some tribes pierced their ears, nose, and lips to wear pearls. Except for painting their faces, men strutted naked, while women discreetly wore palm skirts, frond vests, otter skins (soon to be eradicated because of their value to Russian traders), and nets. The seventeenth-century Jesuit, Father Taraval, wrote, "I can affirm that of all the nets I ever saw in Europe and New Spain, none are comparable to these, either in whiteness, the mixture of the other colors, or the strength and workmanship, in which they represent a rich variety of figures." Nets—woven from palm, mescal, or finer grasses—were also used for fishing and carrying babies. The Californians were skilled weavers and their intricately woven baskets were used for carrying water, or for roasting seeds by spinning them quickly over fires to prevent singeing.

Although the Californians resembled archaic Paleolithic people, and although they were not the noble savages of European myth, they were innocents compared to the sanctimonious Spaniards. The Californians did not drink alcoholic beverages. Two tribes with an imbalance of women did become polygamous, but the men were otherwise protective of women and intolerant of adultery visited upon them by foreigners. Contrary to legends propagated by avaricious Spaniards, the Californians were not cannibals and were so repelled by the idea of eating human flesh that they spurned badger as food because its paw print resembled a human track.

They could look at another's footprints in the sand and tell whom the track belonged to. They caught fish barehanded. They hunted with boomerangs, flint arrows, and fishing hooks. To kill deer, the hunter drew in his prey by holding a dead deer head over his own. To fish, they regularly paddled their reed rafts miles out to sea (which Deborah and I rarely undertake in our fiberglass kayaks). And custom dictated that hunters would be disgraced if they ate their prey instead of giving it to the tribe.

In April 1687, the Jesuit Father Eusebio Francisco Kino and

Admiral Isidoro de Atondo landed in La Paz to attempt yet another California settlement. The long-abused Guaycuras were suspicious and hostile toward these men, who seemed to want more than just pearls. So Kino invited their leaders to a feast, then Atondo fired a cannon into their midst, killing ten Guaycuras. The town of "Peace" was abandoned before the survivors could retaliate.

Atondo sailed north. By October, he and Kino built their settlement, San Bruno, several miles inland. Over the next two years, Kino converted thousands of Cochimi to Christianity. He found the Californians to be "alert" and open to discussing the mysteries of religion. But the lack of fertile soils, an eighteen-month drought, and scurvy among the Europeans made Atondo and Kino withdraw.

Ten years later, the portly Father Juan María de Salvatierra visited San Bruno. The drinking water was brackish and thistles guarded the only remaining wall of Kino's former church. Salvatierra and the others drew lots, and although Salvatierra was tired of long journeys, the paper drawn directed them to continue north.

In October 1697 they arrived at the middle of the peninsula and named it Loreto. They lowered their anchor, filled up on freshwater, and let their animals out to graze. Salvatierra wrote to a colleague:

> many people came to the beach, also women, and there was very merry gossip, at which the natives laughed very much. The males were entirely naked; the women from the waist down to below the knees wore ropes very lightly woven with reeds, and other similar ropes, which made a lot of noise when they moved, like the husking of corn; and as no one had seen suckling pigs, they received much attention.

Salvatierra thought the Cochimi "covetous" of the European maize—causing a rebellion, but undoubtably other unmentioned transgressions against the Indians stirred the unrest.

Salvatierra put them down with guns and eventually became known as the "Jesuit conqueror of California." Other missions were started. Souls were saved. And the Jesuits ruled for seventy-one years under a royal edict that would supposedly prevent soldiers and pearlers from exploiting Californians.

Pearls, in fact, drew many Spaniards to the peninsula without Jesuit supervision and it was these rapacious soldiers and pearlers who taught the Californians mass murder and revenge. In 1712, some pearlers in San José del Cabo arbitrarily executed four Pericú. The next year the Pericú avenged themselves. They coyly asked another crew of pearlers for a show of marksmanship and the Spaniards vainly discharged their single-shot harquebuses into the sky for the Pericú, who quickly killed thirteen Spaniards, sparing only one soldier, Juan Díaz, so they could learn how to sail the pearling ship.

Juan Díaz was ridiculed by these Pericú on a daily basis. Weeks later he escaped by fleeing into the territory of the Guaycura, feared by the Pericú. Although Díaz expected to be killed, the Guaycura fed and cared for him for six months. When a passing ship appeared off the coast, the Guaycura lit a signal fire and released Díaz to his countrymen.

In the mid 1700s, Father Joseph Baegert spent several years in a region where the natives were widely considered "intelligent and peaceful." But Baegert described them as

> stupid, dull, stubborn, dirty, uncouth, ungrateful, lying, knavish, extremely lazy, great gossips, and inasmuch as their intelligence and their activity permit, they remain children to the grave; they are a people who are disoriented, awkward, improvident, rash; a people who can never be tamed and who obey their natural instincts, like the animals.

Baegert then contradicted himself, adding, "They have reason and intelligence like other people, and in my opinion if they were directed from infancy by Europe . . . they would progress in manners, arts and sciences." This from a German who wrote with great detail on the flora and fauna of California, referring to the thorny landscape as "the curse of the Lord . . . after the fall of Adam."

The Spaniards showed the heathens that the terminal buds of the sky duster palms were delicious. Then sky dusters began disappearing because harvesting the bud kills the tree. Nonetheless, palm trees eventually flourished on the peninsula because missionaries planted hundreds of date palms—now a staple crop of Baja California.

The pitaya cactus was one natural crop the Jesuits tried to suppress. The Jesuit Barco wrote that the peach-sized fruit of the pitaya is "so fresh and juicy, it is food and drink at the same time, therefore those who eat a lot of it need little to drink."

The Pericú indians awaited the harvest of the pitaya with great glee and the fruit was treasured like no other food. Their favorite period of their six-season calender was *meyibo,* during the summer pitaya harvest. Another tribe spoke of "this year" as *ambia* (pitaya). As they glutted themselves with pitaya, they jitterbugged in celebration. Father Baegert wrote:

> Their dances consist in a foolish, irregular gesticulating and jumping, or advancing, retreating, and walking in a circle. Yet they take such delight in these amusements that they spend whole nights in their performance, in which respect they much resemble Europeans, of whom certainly more have killed themselves during Shrovetide and at other times by dancing, than by praying and fasting. These pastimes, though innocent in themselves, had to be rigidly interdicted, because the grossest disorders and vices were openly perpetrated by the natives during the performances.

During pitaya orgies, the fruit was so revered in a land of such meager sustenance that the people defecated on rocks. After the pitaya remains dried, the unaltered seeds were plucked out and toasted. The Indians presented the naïve Father Francisco María Píccolo with flour pounded from the seeds, and the father baked bread with it. The more vigilant missionaries met with their colleague and smelled this peculiar bread, making Píccolo the brunt for unending jokes and an enduring "Second Harvest" legend.

Despite the presence of the Jesuits, who built twelve missions, then introduced agriculture, livestock, music, religion, and language to the heathens, California remained a remote and lawless frontier. For all of the piousness of the Jesuit fathers, these eighteenth-century men of the cloth could be as barbaric as the Californians. The padres' stance toward "satanic" witch doctors typified how men of the cloth punished malcontents within their flocks. Dominican Father Luis de Sales, who spent many years on the frontier during the Jesuit reign and started his own mission near the border, wrote:

I have asked one of these witch-doctors whom they call Guaylipai if he felt heat, cold and hunger, if he will die like the rest, and he replied to me: absolutely no; then I ordered a soldier to make a move as if to kill him with the sword through his chest; and on seeing this action the old man began to scream and to flee; afterwards they caught him and gave him some lashings, asking him beforehand if would feel the pain, and he said no; and it made no difference when he was given two or three lashings for he began to scream and shriek like a madman.

Of all the many Jesuit writings, Father Juan de Ugarte, Salvatierra's successor, may have been the least judgmental. While sailing toward the Colorado River, Ugarte and his men needed drinking water. They made hand signs to some Cochimi on the beach. Ugarte described the encounter:

[T]o assure us even more that they understood, they sent forth a young man, and without coming near the ships through fear, he swam with one hand, and with the other gathered water of the sea as if to drink it, pointing to the women who came with drinking water; I could not keep from thinking of this and other cases I had experienced among the heathen of California, showing courtesy, humanity and much ability.

More than two centuries later, Deborah and I have spurned the trappings of our own culture in order to live simply. Because I can only imagine how the Cochimi and the Pericú lived, because my instincts are buried beneath a tidal wave of modern technology and logic, it has taken a lot of letting go (of job, home, and normal routines) to be lying here naked, curled close to my spouse on a bed of warm rocks. I wonder about fire under the earth. I wonder about a sea of saliva, about a rain of tears. Then the dawn comes with the abruptness of a breaching whale as the stars dive into the day and the sun swims above the sea—spitting up shells below.

13

Swimming Birds, Flying Rays

A rising killer whale—A shrine separate from the real church—Bird Island—Contemplating a migraine

Stingrays jump four feet out of the water. They flap and their wings rustle like a cross between a great blue heron and how the leathery-winged pterodactyl must have sounded. But these three-foot rays—related to sharks—crash straight back down in belly flops, a wave of water apostrophizing each flight attempt. Although biologists theorize that rays jump to remove parasites, or to give birth, rays surely watch the shorebirds. Since coyotes imitate sheep, monkeys imitate men, and cormorants imitate fish, why wouldn't rays imitate birds?

As the rays jump, a killer whale rises once, exhales quickly, and slips back under without splashing the white-capped current. I take out the camera but the whale doesn't reappear, and the rays jump unpredictably. I can't swing the camera off my chest fast enough to photograph a jumping ray.

And stopping too long in this current is an invitation for traveling back north.

While paddling around points of land the incoming tide rushes through with all the headlong swish of a river. We often paddle crosswise to it, setting up ferry angles rather than attacking it straight on. We rest ashore.

Near Isla Alcatraz we sift through the remains of an isolated Mexican fishcamp, with a wooden toilet amid a trash dump, three upended refrigerators (miles from a plug-in, but insulating the catch from the heat), arm-sized thresher shark tails, shark jaws, fish bones, and empty store-bought cans of dorado—these fishermen must not eat their catch. A jackrabbit darts through the mesquite.

On the bluff above is a two-foot-high cement shrine—more dollhouse than mosque. Inside are four glass candles, a plastic Mary, and hundreds of rat stools. Outside is church: the Bay of Guadalupe rears back for miles in a sandy curl of saguaro cacti and rolling dunes; to the east the turquoise sea unfurls in white wind caps, pouring between the peninsula and the sixty-mile-long, mountainous Isla Angel de la Guarda. The brown uninhabited land appears disconnected from the sea, rising above it in a shimmering bleached-brown zeppelin of air, more mirage than island.

On Isla Alcatraz hundreds of birds trumpet in raucous symphony; I don't belong. Up on the spine of the hundred-yard islet boobies whistle pathetically, as if pained. Cormorants beat the water with their wings and splash along the surface for fifty yards before gaining flight. Pelicans fly off in a muscular show of wings *whooshing* against air. Western gulls circle round and round and round, defecating and squawking at my intrusion; I cup my ears. The islet is dappled white with bird guano and smells like a fresh-plowed field. I trip over a yellow oil can and catch myself on a truck tire, then leave quicker than I came, vowing never to step on a bird island again.

Deborah has a migraine headache and she thumps the kayak with her hands against the pain. She yells at me for not helping her, but from previous experience I know I can't help until the demerol begins to numb her pain. I give her ten minutes alone.

A doctor might tell her the headache is from dehydration, but I have my own crazy theory. She lies down on the sand, clenching her fist under her nose, eyes shut tight against the double vision. I come back to her and say that I love her and rub her feet as she moans, writhing on her back, while I indulge my theory about how the sea has been violated and maybe we're taking on its pain.

As man's relationship with the natural world crumbles in front of us, our own relationship—clinging to this raft of love—seems our only chance of survival. Without each other we would be lost on a dying sea.

Deborah holds my hand almost tight enough to crush it.

We paddle into a rising tide through the Canal of Whales, smooth as a frozen lake. Turtles frequently break the mirrored tension, and as they pull their beaks back under, target-shaped ripples indent the reflection.

A kingfisher rattles in harmonic accompaniment to its erratic, dipping flight; a coyote pokes along the briny littoral, smells us, then glides into spiny ocotillo thickets.

Beside the volcano-coned, brown-washed Smith Island whales surface and three breaths sound across the waters again and again, like gentle foghorns. I take out my binoculars, but while the acoustics are superb, the distances are vast. The whales are miles off and I can't see them. So I admire the fish flashing green and black and yellow below in this clear, still embryo of life. While listening to the echoing suck and blow of whales, I close my eyes and their vaporous breathing could be the lungs of the sea itself. Hours pass; I don't know how many. Although the sea looks fixed, we have traveled a scant four miles against the hidden tide. We pull ashore to rest and wait for the tide to fall. I read from Steinbeck's *Log from the Sea of*

Cortez while curled in the shade of my sail. Deborah sleeps beside me, her warm breath caressing the hairs on my arm—*this is what I came here for.*

As the tide drops, the north wind comes. I pull up the sail and we link our boats together, gliding past Isla Smith, around past Punta Gringa, and into the fifteen-mile-wide Bahía Los Angeles. "The very air here is miraculous," Steinbeck wrote, "and outlines of reality change with the moment." Thousands of teacup-sized stingrays scatter before us like underwater butterflies as boobies dive in and swim with the fish, and ray wings rustle with air.

14

Supremacist Fishermen

*Steinbeck impressions—Truth or paranoia?—White scorns
black: an old story*

In 1940, John Steinbeck observed that the town of Bahía Los
Angeles had some strange secrecy. He told excited Mexicans
and gringo sportfishermen there that his crew was looking for
marine specimens; suddenly he got the cold shoulder as if they
had expected him to be someone else. Steinbeck thought that
the town was hiding something: gunrunning, maybe gold.

Deborah and I meet some locals who explain that the
town's airport is used by dope-smuggling planes, buzzing the
town late at night to refuel before flying on to El Centro. Apparently, one of Bahía Los Angeles's high-ranking officials was
ousted because he accepted two hundred dollars from every
smuggling pilot. We get more advice: look out for Uzi-armed
smugglers on deserted beaches, gulls pecking open fresh water
bags, and coyotes stealing food. Truth and paranoia become in-
termixed; Mexico is rife with myth. Best to nod your head, lis-

ten politely, thank the teller, practice caution, then let the truth have its way later.

For people willing to drive a full day from the border down a dead-end highway, Bahía Los Angeles has a natural history museum, a half-dozen motels, five small grocery stores (water costs two dollars per gallon, so we fill up for free at the town well), dozens of fishing guides, RV trailer parks, miles of white-sand beaches, and dozens of restaurants. Like most sublime peninsula destinations, this town is yet another symbiotic stew of gringo tourists and Mexican entrepeneurs.

We meet two post-college-age Riverside, California, guys and watch as a Mexican guide fillets their catch of thirty-one tuna: fifteen to twenty-five pounds each. "The fishing hasn't been this good down here in years," one of them explains, "and we got lucky!" I ask if there is a fishing limit and his answer—"Probably, but no one cares"—strikes to the heart of the Sea of Cortés's demise. Their fillets will not fit into two huge coolers.

Tomorrow is our first wedding anniversary and although we would be happier on a deserted beach, we plan to explore Bahía Los Angeles, socialize, and eat some celebratory meals. While shading beneath one of the palapas after dinner, I chat with a kind-faced merchant marine at an adjoining table about his idea for a children's marine biology center across the bay. He's from Philadelphia, the first black man I have seen on the peninsula, and his female companion is from San Francisco. They are both polite and as curious about our journey as we are of theirs. They are here to escape the pressures of career and relax alongside the sea.

At another table, gray-bearded Alta Californians are drunkenly arguing about fish. I can't hear the sea above the clamor, but seeing its white line of foam rinsing up to the tables seems consolation enough. No one seems to mind the unusually fetid smell of ocean.

One of the fishermen shouts: "Pufferfish are NIGGERS: neither of 'em have one iota of intelligence!" and I am so shocked and abruptly removed from the sea that I wonder if I heard wrong. The merchant marine gets up and walks over to the fisherman's table. I am on my feet because the man is alone, the restaurant is silent, and if anyone but the merchant marine feels this outrage they aren't showing it. I stand close enough that the delicate-boned merchant marine knows he has backup.

"Don't you ever talk that way again," he says and I watch the table of six fishermen closely. "What gives you the right to talk that way?" The fishermen are speechless. The merchant marine is beside himself, stamping his foot as he talks because for just a day he thought he was in a country where people didn't care about the color of his skin, because the wilderness of desert and sea had promised only beauty, and because he has lost yet another safe port. For a moment the swirl and suck of the sea is all that anyone can hear until my friend says, "This place is too good for you" and whirls on his heel.

I watch him walk back and as he sits, I address the fishermen loudly: "I didn't come here to listen to good people being slurred and I have no doubt that if it came to a vote, that everyone here would ask this man to leave" and as I point at the shirtless graybeard clutching an empty margarita he comes alive with insults, as if the merchant marine didn't deserve a reply, but now he is ready to fight. He is bluffing. He is a big cocksure, bulging bully. "You're not a fighter, you're a selfish coward, a racist, and an asshole" I say, then rejoin Deborah.

From the adjoining table, the merchant marine manages a wan smile and a nod. His hands are shaking. So are mine.

"Can't get away from 'em, can you?" I ask.

"It's the condition of the world—history repeating itself."

"I had hoped that it was different down here."

"Maybe not, but thanks for what you did," he says.

Then the fisherman walks up, avoiding the man he insulted. In lieu of an apology he comes up and claps my shoulder as if our mock fight has forged some perverse bond between us. He shouts in my ear: "I hope everyone catches plenty of fish tomorrow!"

15

Eighteenth-Century Bigotry

Revolts of the 1730s—The tale of Fabian—French disease ravages the population—Expulsion of the Jesuits—A brief lesson in an extinct language

The ethnic cleansing of Baja California began in the 1730s. An influential witch doctor in the village of Anica incited his people to revolt, an Indian governor named Boton was removed from his office for "misconduct" by the Jesuits, and a mulatto on the Cape, Chicori, became enraged when the fathers refused to return one of his baptized wives.

Father Taraval wrote that the Indian uprising was caused by "dislike of divine precepts and love of barbaric liberty." He heard of the Pericú plotting to kill the missionaries, and warned the soldierless Jesuits, Tamaral and Carranco, who refused to leave their missions. So in September 1734, both Fathers Tamaral and Carranco were murdered by angry Californians—spurred on by Chicori, Boton, and the witch doctors. Father Taraval fled his Santa Rosa Mission in Todos Santos, canoed out to Isla Espíritu Santo, and was eventually rescued by soldiers.

Paddling beside Taraval on that trip was a Pericú named Fabian, who followed Taraval and acted as the father's right-hand man. The rebels repeatedly tried to coerce Fabian to join their cause, threatening to kill his family, but Fabian remained loyal to the Jesuits. As Father Taraval wrote, "From it all he emerged safely and successfully; from each expedition he seemed to derive more courage and even to achieve greater loyalty, fidelity, and zeal."

Fabian served as an interpreter and guide for three years with the Spanish soldiers, fighting several skirmishes with the rebel Indians, who threw rocks and shot arrows while the soldiers blasted away with cannons and harquebuses.

After pitched battles, the Spanish forgave the rebels, offering them food and confession. Fabian watched patiently as the very Indians he had battled against were later pampered, only to again resume their perfidy, while Fabian and his pious, dark-skinned family were treated as vassals and inferiors by the soldiers and Jesuits.

Everything changed when Fabian's wife was taken. The savagery of seventeenth-century Spaniard soldiers is well documented, but Father Taraval was so indifferent to the plight of his loyal companion that the racism and indigenous abuse can be read between the lines—substitute *lured off his wife* with "raped," *abused* with "whipped," and *mistreated* with "severely beat." Taraval's diary is inexplicit:

> What made him [Fabian] turn was the fact that, not content with acting in this wise, the soldiers *lured off his wife* and, when he remonstrated, treated him like an impostor. When he became angry they *abused* him; when he attempted to intercede they *mistreated* him [italics mine].

Fabian left the mission and told his people what had happened to his wife. He reported on the weaknesses of the soldiers and how the rebels might successfully attack each of the occupied missions. Then Fabian returned and freed his tribe's women—who had passively succumbed to the Spaniards' offer of food and shelter. While escaping, Fabian was shot with arrows but he continued to fight, surrounded on both sides. After being shot three times, he surrendered. He was bound up, returned to the mission, and sentenced to the gallows on August 8. Taraval watched the hanging, then finished his evening diary by candlelight:

> He died finally with many unusual indications of being a devout Catholic, repentant and contrite. All this clearly illustrates the wise and pertinent adage of a certain learned man that "God never wields the sword of justice except with the right hand of mercy."

By January 1737, the remaining leaders of the rebellion were either killed in battle or taken onboard ship, carried away, and shot. The insurrection was quelled. On the peninsula, the Spanish victory over the Indians was a microcosm of Cortés's conquest on the mainland because the Spanish did not win by superior battlefield skills. They won by disease.

On the mainland, the first epidemic is traced to a black slave, Francisco de Eguia, who brought smallpox from Africa to New Spain in 1520. Cortés may have been a tactician, but smallpox was his best ally, demoralizing the Aztecs and allowing him to sweep through Tenochtitlán on August 13, 1521. While the seventeenth-century Jesuits were still trying to get a toehold on California, up to 97 percent of the population, or as many as 5 million Indians, died on mainland Mexico.

Seventeenth-century Mayans wrote about the days before 1519:

> There was then no sickness; they had no aching bones; they had then no high fever; they had then no smallpox; no stomach pains; no consumption. . . . At that time people stood erect. But then the *teules* [con-

quistadors] arrived and everything fell apart. They brought fear, and they came to wither the flowers.

The epidemic that ravaged California was known as the French disease (syphilis), introduced by Spanish (or passing European sailors) molesting Californian women. The epidemic could only be passed by sexual contact, or congenitally, from parents to their children. Symptoms were manifested in ten days to ten weeks, beginning with small ulcers and lesions, then "eating away at the groin," and eventually progressing to severe pain until, as the sixteenth-century physician Girolamo Frascastoro described it, "a pustule resembling the top of an acorn, and rotting with thick phlegm, opens and soon splits apart flowing copiously with corrupted blood and matter." The disease feeds upon the body and leaves "joints stripped of their very flesh, bones rotting, and foully gaping mouths gnawed away, the lips and throats producing faint sounds."

Father Baegert wrote about his inland flock, well known for their passivity to the soldiers:

> The patience of Californians in sickness is really admirable. Hardly a sigh is heaved by those who lie on the bare ground in the most pitiable condition and racked with pain. They look without dread upon their ulcers and wounds, and submit to burning and cutting . . . with as much indifference as though the operation were performed on somebody else. It is, however, an indication of approaching death when they lose their appetite.

The Jesuits attributed the epidemic to the devil; shouldering the blame themselves would have been devastating. Referring to the unrepentant Californians, Father Taraval wrote:

> Upon the others God at last inflicted ulcer, fistulas, and incurable cancers so that when their friends saw that their arts were fruitless, they would not believe

nor have faith in them, and the fathers, by making use
of this situation, could then win their confidence.

By 1762, nearly forty thousand Californians had died. Jesuit
fathers died too, beginning at thirty-eight years of age. When
syphilis became fully understood years later, blindness was
identified as a common symptom. In 1746, the most trusted soldier during the uprising, Rodriguez Lorenzo, died after two
years of blindness; his son died four years later of undisclosed
causes, unrelated to a battle. That same year, forty-three-year-
old Father Antonio Tempis also died of undisclosed causes. And
in 1748, Father Clemente Guillen died blind.

Smallpox, originally introduced from a piece of contaminated cloth traded to the Indians by a Spanish sailor, also reduced the California people. In the colonies of America at this
time, the English took action when the Indians contracted
smallpox. The predecessor to inoculation, called variolation,
saved thousands of Indians and colonists in America. But variolation was never practiced in California.

In 1768 the king—acting on suspicions that the Jesuit
church was accumulating vast wealth and would soon over-
throw the throne—expelled the remaining sixteen Jesuit fathers
from California. To this day, most historians laud the Jesuits for
their compassion and accept the writings of people like Father
Baegert at face value:

> To [Californians] the departure seemed a punishment,
> which it actually was; and because of it they, like mil-
> lions of others, did not know what to say or think
> about the affair. On February 3, all of us met in front
> of the beautiful image of the Virgin in Loreto; she was
> clothed in black in mourning as if it were Black Fri-
> day. In spite of the fact that the departure should have
> taken place secretly, all the inhabitants of both sexes
> gathered in the plaza to say goodbye to us, all weep-
> ing, both Californians and Spaniards.

Before the century ended, California Governor Don Pedro Fages wrote:

> That the Missions have deteriorated is beyond question. San José Santiago, Todos Santos, San Javier, Loreto, San José de Comondu, Purisima, Concepción, Guadalupe and Santa Rosalía de Mulegé with giant strides are going to total destruction. The reason is so clear that it cannot be doubted. The disease syphilis ravages both sexes and to such an extent that the mothers no longer conceive, and if they do conceive, the young are born with little hope of surviving.

The Dominicans and Franciscans, who were authorized to replace the Jesuits, avoided the infertile soils and disease-barren peninsula and instead traveled north, to Alta California. By the beginning of the twentieth century, the Pericú and Guaycuras were extinct, and the few remaining Cochimi were moved not to reservations, but to hard labor in chintzy border towns.

The Jesuits' teachings, beginning in 1697, certainly enlightened some of the fifty thousand Indians. According to the Jesuit fathers, many Indians were gifted musicians and singers, requiring little training. Yet by 1790 it was all for naught because only 3,234 Californians survived—to face another epidemic: dysentery. According to the Jesuits, of course, the remaining Indians were said to have mourned the expulsion. But language is a more accurate gauge of history here, and Father Baegert had taken the trouble to transcribe the Guaycuran tongue. Guaycurans had no specific words for the mission employees, so they substituted words meaning "bearers of canes"—with which they were whipped. For *Spanish captain* they substituted "wild" or "cruel." For God they had no word so they were forced to substitute the Spanish *Dios.*

If there was any event approaching a miracle in eighteenth-century California as the Jesuits sailed away, it would have been a Guaycuran uttering in a soon-to-be extinct tongue: "Irimanjure pe Dios"—"I believe in God."

16

Doldrums of Bahía Los Angeles

Tidal potpourri—Wedding anniversary—Sinking to an abyss—Spinner dolphins

Deborah and I pull our tent back above the effluent of Bahía Los Angeles's high tide. Even gulls pass up the offal. Rotted intestines, pelican droppings, nylon leader, a hip boot, plastic bags, a dead stingray, fishhooks, and a condom all bake under the sun in a Sea of Cortés potpourri. The palapas of Guillermos Motel and Restaurant lie fifty yards away, but no amount of money or luxury (the rooms are concrete hovels with seawater showers and blackened toilets) could replace the privilege of sleeping beside the nurturing breath of the sea—even if it is coughing up a few germs.

I give our wedding anniversary my best shot, but Deborah knows I am pretending. We start walking into town, but I convince her that I need to go back to the tent and fix some coffee. Of course she's angry and has every right to be. It's our wedding anniversary and I'm acting indifferent, if only because

I'm exhausted. We probably fight as much as most couples, but the stress of our journey is straining our relationship, subverting our communication.

I write in my journal:

Deb had a fit about the ugliness of our camp and i fell into depression. i refused to go out to dinner and then dropped the bomb and told her that i couldn't take the fighting anymore and maybe we should go our separate ways. This made Deb madder and more resolute, while i fell into an even blacker hole.

My depression is not clinical or manic or much more than a passing black cloud that can rain on anyone, but today I free-fall into an abyss deeper and darker than that of the sea. The fighting with Deborah, the racist fisherman, the stinking tide, the knowledge of history's cycles—or a combination of it all has my head spinning. Whatever its cause, the ache is so profound that I wish it were a migraine so I could just give myself to some pain. I wish it were even hotter so I could sweat myself dry.

Deborah comes back from a long walk, no longer angry, but I beg her to leave me; she does, reluctantly. Zippering myself back inside the torrid tent, I close my eyes and wonder how it would feel, sticking the fish knife up under my ribs and bleeding out into the sea. Where would I go? Where is journey's end? It is not white and it is not up in the sky but closer to the leavings of the tide outside the tent gulping seawater into my lungs and being made to feel the world by bumping up against it with my torso and seeing only blackness and smelling bloodsalt and tasting metal with a hairy tongue. It would be like the horror of trying to sit up to wake yourself from a dream—only to discover that the dream is unwakable death.

I imagine the knife swallowed by my chest and how badly I would regret it, then trying to pull it out too late and if I would have the courage not to scream.

Deborah comes back, scared about what she had seen in

my eyes, and only then do I know its terrible wrongness, so she jumps in, urges me from my torpor, and holds me: shaking and sweating—terrified that I would contemplate leaving her. Without her, I cannot face the journey; without her, I cannot find my strength. I begin mouthing words for an apology.

The first plover whistles *pee-ooooo-wee,* and the filth of the beach, the smell of toilets flushing into the sea, and the attitudes of so-called sportsmen are like waking from another bad dream. Deborah feels sick from last night's dinner. Our best hope is to leave before two dozen *pangas* roar out, loaded with gringos clutching meat rods.

We paddle several miles straight into the gloom-lit bay. The current pulls Deborah a hundred yards south.

I am still baldly self-absorbed and recovering from last night's funk when a sound like a sudden curtain of wind comes from behind. I look back: over a hundred spinner dolphins are splashing toward me. I blink. Town has vanished. The light is unripened apricot, while sky and sea merge. Adult dolphins are bouncing half out of the water while several subadults are jumping completely free. Their snorkeling gasps for oxygen and sprays of carbon dioxide mixed with sea leaves a quick, mysterious scent in the air—like passing a hay field—as they dive under my boat then surface forty feet in front of the bow, gently, so my boat won't be upset but close enough so that we can look at one another. Their wake rocks my boat. They are as curious of me as I am of them, and they could have avoided me, but something drew them in and I am thankful for it.

Their forms shrink smaller and smaller against the rocky arm of Punta Herradura. I cock my head and listen, half-convinced that their high-frequency chatter or sonar whistles will come if I strain hard enough—but there is only animal-swept water luffing against fiberglass. I watch their bodies disappear until all that is left are their vaporous breaths, shooting up like quick, pungent flowers above the sea.

17

Garments of God

*Nausea—A failed marketing ploy—Meeting San Diegoans—
Meeting a cephalopod—Testing theology*

Deborah holds her head over the side of the boat until we must pull over. We are taken in by an uninhabited, two-mile-long, white-sanded, aquamarine-watered bay, Bahía Pescador. Inaccessible by road, it is still blemished by fifteen plywood-sided, palm-thatched cottages. I fix Deborah peppermint tea with honey, then walk over to investigate.

A brochure with a Glendale, California, address in the kitchen palapa advertises this beach as "Agua Verde," a paradise symposium center at which executives can leave the real world behind. Hamburger is rotted into a maggoty gray mass, a letter from a bank is postdated 1990, and coyote tracks dimple the sand. Freshwater barrels and trash on the shore show that Mexican fishermen have been camping on the beach, and consequently, the various kitchen supplies are unlooted.

Two middle-aged, weekend warriors from San Diego, Tom and Glenn, have also kayaked into this (almost) pristine bay. While Deborah dozes in the dusk, I bring some freshly caught pompano—sautéed in garlic and olive oil—to our neighbors for dinner. Tom ladles me "three-can chili" and Glenn fills my cup with Beaujolais. We talk of the state of the sea, its diminishing food chain, its subsequent pollution. Cicadas sing raspily; a coyote yips a long mournful chorus.

Soft-spoken Glenn feels that Mexicans live as Americans did forty years ago, and disposing their trash properly is a low priority next to eking out a living and caring for family. Tom is long-winded, an architect retired upon the strength of his real estate investments, who has been coming to Bahía Los Angeles for a decade.

With no prelude, or perhaps a few too many cups of wine, Glenn announces, in a stilted yet well-educated staccato: "Tom here is gathering his life together because he has a virulent form of cancer and knows, in all probability, that he'll soon be dead."

After an awkward pause I ask: "What kind of cancer?"

"Prostate," Glenn says.

"Glenn is a good ophthalmologist," Tom adds, "but he's not a urologist." He digresses by talking about our beach as "heaven on earth," lamenting how drug money has plopped an eyesore in its middle. "All wrong," he says, "they should've used native materials instead of plywood."

I can't stay. Deborah is sick, and since she needs my attention, I thank them for their company, wishing there was more to do than wish Tom good luck.

She is curled in a fetal position inside the sleeping bag; her forehead leaves sweat against my palm. She is sulking because I left her alone. I thought she was sleeping; she felt abandoned; she pushes me away.

I take the fry pan down to the water. The tide has not dropped this low for more than a month and the seldom-exposed littoral has a rich brininess that makes a sushi bar smell dead in comparison. Although the moon is a sanguine sliver, the shoreline is softly lit by stars reflecting off the sea. While cleaning the pan, I set the pompano skin on a rock a few inches above the water. As the fish and olive oils drain into the water, two octopi, accompanied by tiny black damselfish, jet forward to the edge of their universe. With great deliberation, one forearm-sized octopus slithers out of the water onto the rock, fixing me with a myopic brown eye sensing light, distance, color, and movement. Rolling off Medusa's head like a gelatinous tribe of green polka-dotted snakes, right under my hand holding the fry pan and with more certainty than a skulking gull, it absorbs the fish skin.

Its eight arms, contemplative eyes, and bird beak make it the most unlikely being imaginable. The octopus's cephalopod ancestors lived in multichambered shells under the sea, before humans and even fish, several hundred million years ago. Preyed upon by the many strange and now archaic creatures that could break those shells, the octopus of today abandoned its shell 200 million years ago. Its ancestral cephalopod fossils were deposited on the interior peninsula when the sea receded, enlivening the desert with many thousands of ancient and unlikely forms. The remaining celphalopods (10,500 species are extinct) are among three of the most highly evolved forms of animal life on the planet, including vertebrates and insects. The surviving octopus substitutes speed for shelter, uses reasoning, and shoots out clouds of black melanin pigment that anesthetizes its predators—just as the octopus beneath my hand disappears behind its inky flower, stunning the tiny black reef fish. It shelters beneath a rock, substituting for the curled shell of bygone millennia.

Understanding octopus evolution reveals little about where the ancient cephalopods actually came from. As a species that predates humans by hundreds of millions of years the most important question is *how* did the cephalopod begin? The Jesuits coerced the Californians into believing that God orchestrated a divine moment of creation. Yet this eight-armed and intelligent form is much more real than the modern church's image of God as a bearded, two-legged being dressed in white—more closely resembling an Anglo-Saxon fisherman than a sublime creature of the sea. So why do the architect and the merchant marine suffer, while the fisherman stumbles blithely into old age practicing bigotry? Perhaps the epiphanies of our journey offer the best theology: if there is a God, It will be found in rejecting suicide. It will be found in the perceptive eyes of the octopus, in the gentle tide of a pod of dolphins, and in the life I share with Deborah. I jog up to my wife with a skip and a jump, high as a ray, light enough to fly.

She is silent, glaring, playing her upset stomach for all it's worth—I spent too much time with Glenn and Tom, too much time lost in contemplation of cephalopods, instead of attending her. It's so easy to slip up, to forget to show her the priority she has in my life, so I knead her feet and rave about the octopus until she falls asleep.

I turn to my journal and make words into sentences. My headlamp flickers as I finish the last line: "The miracle of these waters can cure us, even if Bahía Los Angeles is doomed."

18

Cold Light

The origin of Montezuma's Revenge—Shrine below the shrine—Battling around Punta Animas—How to illuminate love

Now we both have Montezuma's Revenge, which is stanched, if not cured, by a dose of Imodium. Mexican Indians consider modern gringo diarrhea not as vengeance for Montezuma (stoned to death by his own people), but for the smallpox and dysentery imported to their country by Europeans, killing millions of sixteenth-century indigenes.

We leave late—9:30 A.M.—and fight every kayak length, making eight miles against the choppy sea and our queasiness.

In Bahía Las Animas we limp above a Mexican fishcamp. A waist-high shrine is filled with the usual gestures of respect: a ceramic Mary, rosary beads bleached pink by the sun, delicate-fringed clamshells and conches, and scallop-shell impressions in cement. We can smell the crapping grounds below; used toi-

let paper, napkins, and newspaper flutter in the breeze. Our stomachs churn.

The sun falls and we push off to take advantage of the sunset calm to cross the bay. A gringo camper lofts a beer, motioning us into his white-sand beach, but we press on in the cross surf, bent on being alone with the sea. We settle for a rocky cove far enough above the water to keep us dry if we leave before dawn's high tide.

Water is churning; an osprey whistles sharply; my face is cold. I open my eyes: no clouds, the sky is clear, but the sea is jumpy. It takes three separate attempts to wake Deborah, and once she is moving, half sick, she packs so slowly that we can't paddle for another hour and a half. We plunge into a chaos of wind and tide. We push on thinking that the other side of Punta Animas will offer calmer waters. Even at slack tide the water twists and turns in disconcerting confusion, so we stare at the land as if fording a river, to avoid getting any dizzier and more frightened. Around the point the water gets bigger, and before I can yell "turn back" it's too late. We're committed.

Now we lose the luxury of focusing anywhere but the whitecapped and breaking waves in order to plan each paddle stroke. Glimpsing Deborah boosts my confidence because her kayak appears to carve into, then crest the waves effortlessly— helping me to visualize the control of my own kayak. Nonetheless, we're on the edge, trying to guess where the waves will break, then thumping our rudders to turn into unpredictable breaks: bursting like sudden thunder in our ears. The shoreline is cliffed, so we stay out at sea to avoid refracted swells. My sphincter clenches with fear, my throat swells with adrenaline, and I try to find that river of psychological calm that will propel us through our biggest water yet; Deborah is screaming the sort of inanities of riders in a plunging roller-coaster car. It is consolation to think that if we tackled such big surf our first day out, we would have simply rolled over and capsized in terror.

Now we are trailing towlines. In case we spill and can't re-board, at least the other kayaker—if one of us remains up-right—can tow the upset boat ashore. Abandoning a boat and its essentials to the sea would force us to walk out over the desert or flag down a fisherman for help, ruining all our dreams of self-sufficiency.

Soon enough, I drop my shoulders, feel digestive juices rushing in my stomach, and let my synapses take over as my mind free-associates:

> *The paddle joint clicking becomes my brother's dislo-cating jaw clicking as he devours hamburgers out on the deck of his Denver home—above fragrant, tart raspberry bushes. All is calm at Jerry's house and I feel light because no effort is required when we're together making up for the lost time from our splintered family, the nine-to-five mundanities and the pressures of ca-reers. At Jerry's house the day-to-day burden of life is lifted.*

A wave washes into my mouth and I realize that I better start concentrating.

We round Punta Piedra San Bernadene and steer south into a bay running fifty times as wide as the Colorado River surging into Lava Canyon—so we sneak alongside the shore in a quieter eddy. We pull out and brew up a liter of coffee.

"You were scared," I taunt her, "weren't you?"

"You bet I was scared, but you kept falling behind!" She jumps on me and pins me in a wrestler's lock. I give up, partly as compromise, but mostly to avoid breaking my arm.

Although we both felt wretched and self-conscious in Bahía Los Angeles, out here we feel perfectly in place. Like the Mexican *panga pescadores* behind us in Bahía Las Animas, we have even abandoned wearing sunglasses. We boast about who is more Cochimi, showing off our tans. A sheen of brine puck-ers and dries up my shoulders, flaking off like dandruff.

A forty-foot yacht is anchored offshore. Since the yachter figures it couldn't be too rough if kayakers came around Punta Las Animas, he weighs anchor and motors out for a try. Within fifteen minutes he retreats back to his safe anchorage. I jokingly suggest that maybe we could hitchhike south for a few days and Deborah growls a reply. So we push off.

Within an hour, the spring tide and the gathering wind whips the sea into maelstrom. I can't see my wife behind the waves, so I shout directions to her, simultaneously turning toward the only calm lagoon for miles. No time for discussion. We wrestle our boats back above high tide line, so shaky-handed and filled with adrenaline that we cannot talk civilly. I try and explain the urgency of exiting quickly, without discussing it out in the surf, but she dislikes being given directions, and she is angry at me for suggesting that we start earlier in the mornings. We yell, but I can see that we'd better drop it.

I angrily bound up a small peak, dodging fat spiders, perched like octopi in labyrinthian webs. Two vultures soar on the thermals; a canyon wren flitters into a stand of pitaya cactus.

Isla Tiburón (shark) appears forty miles away—it's the sea's largest island, thirty-five miles long, twenty miles wide. Isla San Esteban dots the *i* of Isla Tiburón. Out there, for hundreds of years, Seri indians gambled on how close they could ride turtle shells to the edge of a cliff before jumping off. The men who lost plunged to the rocky shore below, forsaking their wives to their opponents; the surviving winners, standing closest to the abyss, were paid in pearls, fish, and feathers. *If only life could be that simple.*

Back in camp, Deborah is still angry. At twilight I land a leathery-skinned triggerfish. I shower sparks onto driftwood, striking the flint as if concurrently whittling wood and lighting sulfur matches: the driftwood smokes; I blow until it writhes alive: a flaming orange inchworm.

I roast the triggerfish wrapped in aluminum foil with carrots and onions on the coals. It's like crab: sinewy and sweet and firmer than any fish. As we chew and sip, light pinpricks the sea, as if the stars are striking sparks into the waters. Coleridge describes it in "Rime of the Ancient Mariner":

> About, about, in reel and rout
> The death fires danced at night
> The water, like a witch's oils,
> Burnt green and blue and white.

A half century later, as Darwin sought to explain the workings of a world too complex for the machinations of a single divine Being, he observed this phosphorescence. After making observations from the bow of his *Beagle,* Darwin wrote in his diary:

> Every part of the water which by day is seen as foam, flowed with a pale light. The vessel drove before her bows two billows of liquid phosphorus, and in her wake was a milky train. As far as they eye reached the crest of every wave was bright; and from the reflected light, the sky just above the horizon was not so utterly dark as the rest of the Heavens.

We now have the luxury of knowing that these cold lights of the sea are caused by microscopic-sized dinoflagellates—half animal because they consume organic matter, and half plant because they benefit from photosynthesis. Enacting the same phenomenon that allows fireflies to produce light, the dinoflagellates have two enzymes—oxidized by passing boats, the surf, or even a churning fish—making the sea burn with cold, starry light.

Wading thigh-deep into now-calm water, I ask my lover to turn off her headlamp in order that I might "show her the light" on this night. I ask, "Will you forgive me for yelling today out in the rough water?"

No reply.

I fill a pot with seawater and twirling with my pot half-tipped like a marionette, I spin the Sea of Cortés in long circles back into itself, splashing round and round, over and over again, thousands of tiny animals—bound to us and the sea and the stars above by time and fate—bursting out in circles and oxidizing into miniaturized, sea-level Milky Ways as Deborah squeals with delight at the wonders of our isolation together, illuminating the night with forgiveness.

Deborah leads me back to the sleeping bag by my hand and we peel off our clothes. I brush my fingertips across her wide cheekbones and wonder how it feels and if we shall ever transcend our own singular needs. Does her nose itch? Is her forehead still burning with the sun? It is her face, not mine; our faces, and for that matter *our souls,* float somewhere apart, but in these moments that we come together the conjoining is finer than any thing or place or person we have touched. If our waters should finally merge during our short time together on this old earth then that is our heaven. We go there, however briefly:

Starlight purls above like creatures glowing in the great black sea of night, and we are otherwise blind, holding and caressing and loving one another as my sadness fades and her anger melts and our world becomes the salt taste of our sea-soaked skin and ancient Colorado River clay in our belly buttons and the storm surf of our own breathing.

A bat chirps birdlike then sleep takes us far, far away from the fragile china of our marriage.

19

The Vermilion Sea

*A surf-battered shore—Oystercatchers—Big water—If you
are going to Bahía San Fransiquito—Paving the
peninsula—Bleeding sea*

We swill cold instant breakfast drink sprinkled with instant coffee like nutmeg on cappuccino. Then we're paddling. Dolphins
jump in front of us, disappear, and the waves sway us into
mindless, timeless rhythm.

We quit on an ivory sand beach. American oystercatchers
balance one-legged next to a marbled godwit. Black-bellied
plovers and semipalmated sandpipers bustle on the sand,
plucking protozoic scraps off the sand between waves. Royal
terns flirt just above the curl of the breakers, performing aerial
half somersaults, just like the sea. Brown boobies turn sudden
jackknifes, throwing up exclamation points of water.

The American oystercatcher has a neon-red bill more than
twice the length of its black head and shaped not unlike an
oysterman's double-edged knife. Their yellow eyes are painted

with red mascara. While early *Bajacalifornios* bandied about an unfortunate pearl diver caught and held under by a giant clam, the Audubon Society claims that exposed clams catch unwary oystercatchers' bills—until high tide drowns the bird.

The rising surf thwarts the oystercatchers, so the trio flies off with powerful short wing beats, issuing a creaky: *crik, crik, crik.* The marbled godwit joins them.

I turn to my journal:

> Where do the birds go when they die? Are they cast off by their companions? Do they fly inland and die? Do they sit on a cactus until they fall over? Or are they eaten?
>
> Where do the animals go when they die? Where do the fish go when they're old? Where do the whales and the dolphins go?

We move our tent back, a full stone's throw from the booming waves so that we can sleep. The sea blasts a cooling salt mist through the air.

Thousands of brown ants run a forty-yard-long fire drill in front of our tent. Deborah throws a tortilla on the other side of their ant hole to assure our privacy in the tent. Deborah's knotted back has tiny nodules, but pinching long and hard dissolves them, until I gradually lighten the touch and she falls asleep. I slip outside.

As the sun dips low and paints the surf spray nectarine, I trace the thorny trunk of a ten-foot-tall saguaro cactus with my fingertips—gentle as touching my wife's back—which prevents me from being spined by unseen, hairlike glochids, and allows me to feel the velvety white fringe, softer than fleece, cleaner than snow. Amazing what a caress can reveal.

The surf is still up. Eight seconds elapse between wave sets, so after the last set, I push my boat, leap in, and paddle over a wave before it breaks. I pull my sprayskirt over the cockpit combing so when a three-footer sputters over my chest, I stay dry.

Deborah waits a few sets, until a rogue wave sucks her boat down into the surf and knocks her down; she snags the bowline, barely saving her boat. After bailing out, she finds the courage to leap in just as an early breaking wave half fills her boat. At least we're both past the breaks; I hand her the bilge pump; she narrows her eyes at me.

She is upset that I entered clean and she didn't. If Deborah and I were not competitive, our relationship might have longer calms between wave sets, but adventuring together in extremis would be harder. Competition drives us. If the skiing gets too steep for me, Deborah jumps in smiling; then I'll follow. If we have to get up a mountain and daylight is fading, we race one another up. If one of us is scared in a precarious place, the other acts confident, until we're both safe again, teasing one another about our weaknesses.

We paddle along the growing troughs, a long spit from their transformation into foaming, breaking waves. It's unnerving on the crest of breakers-to-be, but more predictable than paddling further offshore in wind-whipped, multidirectional water.

As I get confident, my concentration wanes and I drift too far in: a wave breaks over my head with a sudden clapping pushiness. A quick paddle brace to the east prevents me from flipping.

"Paddle further out, *you dummy!*" Deborah yells.

I nod. She's back in control, competing and racing me to the point; catching her will take an hour of swift paddling, *if* she takes a rest.

The waters at the rocky Punta Ballena are a cauldron of conflicting currents, rocking our boats back and forth. Sea lions bark, Deborah yells unintelligibly, and we would be terrified except for three hundred miles of earned familiarity; Deborah sees me plunge in, taking a direct line through the whitewater, and follows. *We will not capsize* goes the mantra in my head.

We even have the luxury of knowing that around the corner, like previous points, the current will drop.

In Bahía San Fransiquito we are transfixed. The sand is the color and consistency of unrefined sugar, arcing for a symmetrical mile and a half, with gentle half-foot-high breakers rising the entire length of the beach as an extended pane of glass before shattering onto sugar. Cliffs block the wind.

The desert's aridity highlights its juncture with the sea. Fish splash; sea lions frolic; the ocean yawns in aquamarine infinity. If beaches could be nominated as ambassadors to speak to the shorelines of the world, this would be Mexico's delegate.

In 1940, John Steinbeck cruised through and wrote:

> A beach of white sand edges this cove, and on the edge of the beach there was a poor Indian house, and in front of it a blue canoe. No one came out of the house. Perhaps the inhabitants were away or sick or dead. We did not go near; indeed, we had a strong feeling of intruding, a feeling sharp enough even to prevent us from collecting on that little inner bay. The country hereabouts was stony and barren, and even the brush had thinned out.

Since the few surviving Cochimi were pushed north, Steinbeck saw Indians hauled over from the mainland to work as vassals in peninsular mines. Today there are as many as two hundred Cochimi scattered through the desolate sierras and dry valleys of Baja Norte. Today Cochimi do not talk to outsiders because they have learned from the past.

Here in Bahía San Fransiquito, a mestizo, or mixed-blood, Mexican family caretakes the fishing lodge. A dozen bungalows lie above the dunes. The air smells of sharp astringent ocean and the sand looks so clean and inviting we want to roll in it. I explain our journey to the husband—a reserved, wiry man of some thirty years. He is incredulous to the point of curiosity: "¿Su esposa kayako, *San Felipe?*"

I flex my biceps and point to Deborah, saying: "¡Mi esposa es muy fuerta!"

Felix laughs and shouts to his own young wife, who puts aside her broom and stares with shining eyes and yellowing teeth at Deborah. Two women, two countries, two decades apart in liberation.

Her five-year-old stands with hand inserted in mouth until she removes it to accept a cookie; she and her bother say "gracias" to Deborah without prompting.

Felix fills our water bags from barrels driven over a rutted dirt track fifty miles from the town of El Arco. He explains that most of the guests, who come for the fishing, fly in small planes to San Fransiquito. Before the Transpeninsular Highway was built in 1971, gringos flew everywhere—evidenced by

scores of dirt strips along the coast. Felix hopes that they will someday pave the road to improve business; we do not mention that paving it might bring the seedy tee shirt shops, squalid taco stands, and litter heaped like feces that we saw in San Felipe and Bahía Los Angeles. In Spanish, *inmensidad* (wilderness) means "a lack of culture"; Felix believes that paving the wilderness will bring it needed culture.

Felix acts vaguely insulted when I offer him some pesos for his difficulty in the drive. He says that where we're going, we need the water more than he does. He laughs. The kids wave. The wife covers her teeth and resumes what appears to be sadness—but for all of our cultural differences, who knows what she really feels?

In Bahía San Juan Bautista we pass through an eerie calm of blood water. At first it seems that a whale has died. The water even smells of death: all fish guts and copper.

A lifeless cormorant floats with a lolling head. Another rises beside the corpse and quickly flies off, slapping the water and dragging its tail until finally gaining air forty yards later. After having watched hundreds of cormorants effortlessly dive away, perhaps the live cormorant was startled by its dead kin rather than by my kayak. We paddle on until it dawns on us that these deep clouds of vermilion are the same animals that glow at night: billions upon billions of blooming dinoflagellates.

Ulloa was the first sailor to describe this "Vermilion Sea" (Mar Bermejo) in September 1539. Many other sailors saw it and consequently, most maps bore this name instead of Cortés's.

Reddened water can also be caused by pelagic shrimp or clays washing out the Colorado River, but whenever the water warms enough for dinoflagellates to feed, the tiny creatures bloom in a diurnal eclipse of their nocturnal glow.

Exodus 7:21 describes a "red tide"—interpreted as God's

punishment of the pharoah for retaining Moses in Egypt—turning a river to blood, killing fish, stinking to high heaven, and preventing the Egyptians from drinking it.

Aboard the *Beagle* Darwin described a bloom without naming the animal or linking it with nighttime phosphorescence:

> [O]ne day passed through great bands of muddy water, exactly like that of a swollen river. Some of the water when placed in a glass was of a pale reddish tint, and examined under the microscope was seen to swarm with minute animaculae darting about and often exploding.

Fifty years ago a Gulf of Mexico bloom half the length of Florida killed 500 million fish. People walking the shore contracted colds and sore throats. Other ruinous "red tides" have clouded shorelines of Alta California, Alaska, New England, Australia, and Bombay—causing fish kills and paralytic shell poisoning in people who ate soft clams or mussels.

Although most dinoflagellates are nonpoisonous, if the floating cormorant is any sort of indicator, the species blooming beneath our paddles is probably the toxic *Goniaulax catenella*. Judging by several *panga*-loads of fishermen working Bahía San Juan Bautista, the Mexicans are unfazed by the red tide. The fragile animals' two flagella legs will break off when a wind starts roiling the sea, sinking billions of red, encysted bodies and clearing the water.

We paddle on through the Vermilion Sea. Blood tentacles the edges of the calm. My shoulders are leaden. All is still, trolling for fish is not an option, and the unexpected pallor of the sea reduces us to funereal silence.

During a quick stop in Santa Rosalía, Deborah stays with the boats and I take four empty water bags to a gas station. Two men in their early twenties help me fill up at a spigot. I refuse to buy or smoke their marijuana and their scam begins. It's an old game: the knowing smiles between two con artists, the questions about how much my trip costs, and their hands bumping against pockets where my wallet might be. Their breath reeks sweetly; it's not pitayas.

Raul and Manuel begin escorting me back to the kayaks, ostensibly to help, but they want something more. At the very least they will harangue me for pesos once we're out of the public eye and on the secluded beach. And for many young Mexican men, switchblades are a badge of honor. Raul and Manuel are hard-timing young mestizos who have no work: spawned by poor mine workers, descendants of conquistador and Indian vassal. *My abduction,* I think, *would be the real revenge of Montezuma.* They take turns clasping my elbows, muttering among themselves, steering me. I'm bigger than either Raul or Manuel and could hold my own, *if* they don't pull blades, but I'm not half as desperate as they are—so I'll pick the arena and the rules.

I get my opening in front of some older locals socializing on the street. I stop, then straighten up from the obvious weight of ten gallons of water. Speaking loud enough so that the crowd can hear, knowing the honesty of most Mexicans, I say, "¡Raul y Manuel, no gracias, vaya pronto!" then watch the eyes of older men raking over the two town *pachuchos.* Their shoulders slump, their mouths drop open, and with a nod of my head, I dismiss them: "¡Adiós!"

20

Silver Lining

Reclining and running—Father Baegert's judgments—
Punta Chivato's "progress"—NAFTA— Electric show

We exit rough waters in a shallow cove; I trip out of my kayak onto hands and knees. The top half-foot of beach is tiny crushed shells—several hundred years removed from sand, several million years removed from gypsum. Almost too sharp to crawl upon. I paw down below and find intact scallop shells. As wavelets roll up the beach, water draws through this shell layer cake, gurgling like a coffee percolator. I press ear to shell-sand and listen: *rrrrrrrrrrrrrrrrrrr.*

Deborah stretches, yawns, and takes off down the beach. Sea kayaking isn't strenuous cardiovascular exercise, but after paddling all day my main interest is reclining on the beach. Nonetheless, running dissipates the competition between us. She fades into a speck of blond hair and brown skin, then disappears down the shoreline as lithe and as fleet-footed as a Californian.

Two centuries ago, Father Baegert wrote about Cochimi runners:

> They will run twenty leagues [fifty miles] today, and return tomorrow to the place from whence they started without showing much fatigue. Being one day on the point of setting out on a journey, a little boy expressed a wish to accompany me, and when I gave him to understand that the distance was long, the business pressing, and my horse, moreover, very brisk, he replied with great promptness: "Thy horse will become tired, but I will not." Another time I sent a boy of fourteen years with a letter to the neighboring mission, situated six leagues from my residence. He started at seven o'clock in the morning, and when about a league and a half distant from his place of destination, he met the missionary, to whom the letter was addressed, mounted on a good mule, and on his way to pay me a visit. The boy turned round and accompanied the missionary, with whom he arrived about noon at my mission, having walked within five hours a distance of more than nine leagues [22.5 miles].

Living close to the sea for a month has shown us a doorway (shelterless Cochimi called church entrances "mouths") into a simpler life. Even in the eighteenth century, Father Baegert observed a difference between his civilized Europe and ascetic California. It was the way of those times to interpret the New World's wilderness as primitive rather than beautiful, to see the cactus thorns rather than the pitaya fruit, and label the undeveloped as satanic rather than ethereal.

Baegert spent a long six years at San Luis Gonzaga Mission (still standing). He cultivated pomegranate, figs, and citrus fruit—making an oasis out of desert. On some level the simple joys of the wilderness must have dented his impenetrable Jesuit armor. He wrote a book, *Account of the American Peninsula of*

California anonymously, perhaps to disown his constant moralizing. He conceded some truths:

> [T]hey live unquestionably much happier than the civilized inhabitants of Europe, not excepting those who seem to enjoy all the felicity that life can afford. Habit renders all things endurable and easy and the Californian sleeps on the hard ground and in the open air just as well and soft as the rich European on the curtained bed of down in his splendidly decorated apartment. Throughout the whole year nothing happens that causes a Californian trouble or vexation, nothing that renders his life cumbersome and death desirable; for no one harasses and persecutes him, or carries on a lawsuit against him; neither a hail storm nor an army can lay waste his fields, and he is not in danger of having his house and barn destroyed by fire. Envy, jealousy, and slander embitter not his life, and he is not exposed to the fear of losing what he possesses, nor to the care of increasing it. No creditor lays claim to debts; no officer extorts duty, toll, poll tax, and a hundred other tributes. There is no woman that spends more for dress than the income of the husband allows; no husband who gambles or drinks away the money that should serve to support and clothe the family; there are no children to be established in life; no daughters to be provided with husbands; and no prodigal sons that heap disgrace upon whole families.

Deborah and I are here because our home life is not unlike Baegert's Europe, removed from the earth by speeding along in our cars, whizzing through the atmosphere in pressurized aluminum tubes, as we acquire more material possessions and saddle ourselves with a mortgage and taxes. We have come to Baja California to escape the rest of our life, inescapable and essential as it may be.

If Father Baegert rode a time machine to the present, the "civilization" of Baja California would provoke his skeptical mind. A few years shy of the twenty-first century, replete with the benefits of computer-driven science and far-sighted technology, Father Baegert would see the light of truth. By pillaging the world's richest sea and overdeveloping its boundaries, he would say, man has become a race of techno-barbarians, oblivious to the omnipresence of God.

We enter a series of sand lagoons and rocky reefs. A dolphin speeds in and blows beside us, guarding its calf. An affable boobie wobbles left and right, trying to balance on webbed blue feet.

American RVs, camper shells, and tents roost on the next beach. Twenty-eight homes are perched along the shore, costing several times that of our thirteen-hundred-square-foot home—it costs $140 per square foot to build here. Unlike other American developments along the Sea of Cortés, there are Montana, Arizona, and Colorado homeowners here, but mostly northern Californians. Satellite dishes abound, as if the sea is not sufficient entertainment.

We have paddled 420 miles. We want to celebrate by washing off the salt and sand, by sleeping under sheets, but the Punta Chivato Hotel is too pricey. We settle for buying dinner. At the bar, gringo and mestizo alike are glued to their stools while an ESPN football announcer yells out of a large television.

We read a recent magazine story about the pending North American Free Trade Agreement. The aim of NAFTA is to remove taxes from goods flowing between Mexico, the United States, and Canada—ultimately creating one continental economy. American industry is being enticed to move to Mexico where environmental laws aren't enforced and local labor costs fifty-eight cents an hour. According to the article, political pundits think NAFTA "is a cloud with a silver lining." The supposed ban of commercial fishing in the northern sea, for instance, was to entice Congress into passing NAFTA. No one knows if Mexico will "green up" and meet American environmental standards. Keeping the air and water clean, saving marine species, and preserving the oceanic chain of life will stretch the Mexican government and its age-old system of corruption.

Back on the beach, the moon throws our shadows and whitens our teeth as we plod nervously to the outhouse (Baegert described reaching for a razor in his bathroom and finding a rattlesnake instead). Heat lightning flashes over the northeastern sea in long illuminating bolts, as if the sky has waged war against the night. Cumulonimbus clouds are stacked miles high, mounting to the stratosphere. No thunder booms. We walk transfixed as a single lightning bolt travels around the edge of a cloud with all the accuracy of a sketching pen, showing us jaded humanoids how strange and wonderful the world is, how fantasy can merge with reality, how natural events can rock your soul and deliver innocence. Deborah puts her arm around me and I time-travel on beyond our footsteps. As the fine white sand percolates through my toes, I imagine us growing old together, standing on a beach on my eighty-fifth birthday, putting my arm around her. It will never work.

We don't speak, but it is plain to see. For a brief and brilliant two seconds the cloud has a silver lining.

21

Machismo

*Downtime—Gringo fishermen loaded to the gills—Paving
Mulegé—The Mexican male tradition*

The banks of Rio Mulegé hold a croaking great blue heron,
semitruck trailer homes, fishing guide shacks, and a deserted
airstrip. I look for the legendary big snook darting in the shadows but they're probably fished out.

Our hands fester with salt sores, we have been eating anti-
inflammatory Motrin pills (for sore backs and necks) like
candy, and despite a huge dinner and breakfast at Punta Chivato, we're still famished. We need a vacation.

We unload our kayaks at the Serinadad Hotel, alongside a
garrulous sportfisherman, winching an eighteen-foot boat onto
his truck trailer. He crows about the six-wheeler's cubic dis-
placement and fish-hauling capacity. He says it's 620 miles and
two days worth of driving back to America. He gestures to one
of two dozen coolers holding twenty-eight-pound blocks of

ice—all built into the pickup bed. I ask how many fish he "slaughtered" over the weekend; he catches the edge in my voice and evades the question. We head to the bar.

How many men go fishing all their lives, Thoreau asked, without ever realizing that the fish were not what they were looking for?

Women are often wiser in these matters than men; women don't fish. Deborah caught a fish two weeks ago only because I handed her the rod (with triggerfish attached) and stepped away. She had to land it and ate its flesh reluctantly. I enjoyed every bite.

Our mustachioed waiter, Sal, moonlights as a guide, and speaks English well. We hire him to take us to the headwaters of the river and show us some ancient cave art. He is thirty years old, a beefy, handsome Mulegé lifer.

A steamroller paves over the old cobbled streets as sad-faced village elders stand by with arms crossed tightly on their chests. It feels like two-point-five on the Richter scale: store-front windows flutter, pottery rattles, and shelves dump their holdings onto floors.

The three-storied Misión Santa Rosalía de Mulegé was re-built on a hill south of town in 1770 after a flood destroyed the 1705 mission on the river. The Rio Mulegé, also called Rio Santa Rosalía, was the peninsula's only year-round river before dams were built to suppress floods and irrigate Jesuit plantings. Sal steers his battered taxi-van east toward the headwaters, past banana trees, date palms, and orange orchards. Sal waves to friends at the thriving ice block factory—yet another product of the river—where several trucks with American plates replenish their coolers.

As we stroll up the canyon, our guide plays naturalist. A flycatcher alights on a nearby rock and Sal calls it "the canyon bird." He points to the chest-high "lonvoi cactus" and says, "You can suck on its fruit if you're thirsty." I snatch one of the balls before Sal warns me that it will take hours to pluck its nearly invisible thorns from my fingers. A roadrunner sprints past us on the trail and Sal solemnly explains the local myth about how roadrunners kill rattlers by encircling cholla cactus thorns around the sleeping snakes.

Sal answers our constant questions with growing irritation. The abundant fingernail-sized toads hopping out of the river pools are "the canyon frogs." The snake slithering away beneath a rock is "the rock snake." The tiny rodents are "canyon mice." A wren flitting atop a cardón cactus is "the cactus bird."

Sal has three children, but he cryptically explains that his wife is young and very unhappy with him. No further explanation is necessary, given Sal's frequent attempts to gaze through the fabric of Deborah's shirt.

Blondes like Deborah are rare south of the border, and to Mexican men, a fair-skinned, blond woman—respectfully referred to as *una güera*—symbolizes an escape from the dark-skinned features of most Mexicans. Although *Bajacalifornios* insist that they're different because the peninsula was settled later than the mainland, the heritage behind Sal's behavior is predictable. Adultery is common here; Mexican men treat women as inferiors.

So the mother becomes the pillar of the Mexican family, raising the children and keeping the family intact when the fathers leave. Despite modern inroads bridging places like Mulegé, the underlying mistrust between men and women prevents me from developing a conversation with most Mexican women in the streets or at the hotel or in the shops. Whether single or married, it is a characteristic of Mexican women to socialize primarily with their own sex.

Sal may be a devoted husband and father, and ogling women may be more sociological phenomenon—that Deborah has observed throughout the peninsula—than imprecation. In Spain, the definition of *machismo* has to do with the preoccupation of defending one's honor. In Mexico, because of the reign of Spanish oppression, machismo has more to do with defending a weak masculinity.

Of course, Sal's furtive glances and obsequious behavior

toward Deborah could be interpreted as nothing more than the genetic impulse, a condition of the male species everywhere. But the crucial difference with Mexico is its conquistador and missionary heritage. Since the Spanish arrived, Indian men witnessed women being raped or taken away, while the dominating conquistador or missionary did not trust the Indians he lorded over. Sal is a mestizo—half Spaniard, half Indian—and his behavior has been encoded by the unalterable events of Mexico's past.

We stop at a pool of cool, green water. Sal says we must swim. He hangs out long enough to watch Deborah strip to her bathing suit and as we swim, our guide walks forty yards along a hidden trail and nonchalantly waits, dry as a frigatebird, while we emerge like cormorants from the pool's far end.

22

Cave Art

Jesuit interpretations of "the giants"—Connection to the sea—Swimming slot canyons—Worshiping painters

After a short hike we arrive beneath the first Trinidad Cave mural. Red and white handprints dapple a high wall, a human figure celebrates with hoisted arms above an inverted deer, a shark lies languid, and an unfamiliar fish is presented as a bony X-ray image—Sal claims it's red snapper, his favorite seafood.

The art was drawn by a race of people referred to as "the giants." Jesuit missionaries named a nearby mountain range Sierra Gigantica after these painters. Hazy legends—supported by the handprints five feet above our heads—were started by the Cochimi. But the eighteenth-century Indians did not know the meaning behind the murals, nor could the Cochimi paint. They assumed that the high paintings had to have been created by giants.

The Jesuits, with their chronic and righteous documentation of all things ethnological, quickly seized upon this discovery as a new race of men. Francisco Clavijero, an eighteenth-century Jesuit historian, wrote in *Storia Della California:*

> Not belonging to the savage and tribal natives who inhabited California when the Spaniards arrived there, these pictures and dresses, without doubt, belonged to a people more ancient and unknown to us. There is a tradition throughout the country that it was a gigantic people who came from the north. We do not claim credit for these traditions, but from various exhumations of human bones by the missionaries it cannot be doubted that formerly the country was inhabited by men of disproportionate size.

The Jesuits were pleasantly surprised to find that these murals depicted giants in clothes, rather than the naked heathens inhabiting California. But the height of the murals alone wasn't enough to launch a myth. In 1765, forty miles north of the Rio Mulegé petroglyphs, Father José Robéa supposedly discovered large skeletal remains near another mural. Based on this thirdhand evidence, Clavijero concluded:

> Taking into consideration the magnitude of the cranium and the place occupied by the whole skeleton, and comparing the vertebrae with those of an ordinary skeleton, it is believed that the man to whom it belonged measured eleven feet in height.

Modern rock art experts concluded that the painters used scaffolding to paint as high as thirty-three feet off the ground. Baja California's four hundred murals and paintings are fifteen hundred years old. Pottery shards are found near the murals; the latter-day Cochimi used only reed and wooden baskets. The form and deliberation behind these paintings is comparable to Anasazi petroglyphs scattered in the American Southwest, or the proliferation of paintings at Lascaux and Altamira in Europe. While the conjectured disappearance of Anasazis in the American Southwest is from drought or war, no one even guesses what happened to "the giants" of Baja California.

The paintings have an extraordinary connection to the sea, even though most murals are inland (we're more than a dozen miles from the sea). The murals depict people, sheep, and deer, as well as sea life. Dolphins and whales are never inverted or "dead," assorted fish are often portrayed upside down, and a bowhunter stalks a manta ray—patently feared by Cochimi and not hunted for food until the advent of the Mexican taco stand.

Approaching the next mural involves swimming up a narrow side canyon. Sal shows the route by drawing a map in the sand, then promptly leaves us, claiming that he is a fine swimmer, but as a hot-blooded Mexican, he cannot tolerate *el agua fría*. We stuff our cameras and clothing in nylon dry bags looped over our shoulders.

As we wade up to our chests, then begin stroking through fresh green water, I suppress the urge to drink—above and below the canyon are hundreds of gaunt and dysenteric-looking Brahman cattle. Our movements ripple the water, reflected clearly on the bottom as yellow concentric bull's-eyes surrounding our bodies. We are silent as churchgoers. Then Deborah mentions freshwater alligators but suppresses giggling until after my eyebrows rise.

Ocher blushes the towering sandstone walls, blackened with ancient rain varnishing or rinsed tawny by floodwaters. The canyon narrows as wide as our outstretched arms; we tread water. A vulture rides an updraft above, and I shiver, just like the giants shivered. We clamber over a small waterfall and onto dry land; palm fronds peek above the canyon floor; a tarantula on a boulder processes the pattern of our passage.

The cave resembles the reddened mouth of a petrified leviathan. Inside, a white whale has been painted at eye level and we imagine the giants' awe as they stood close and admired this behemoth of the sea.

A dolphin is detailed in ocher with its unmistakable smiling beak. *They knew,* I think, *they knew about the intelligence of dolphins.*

With my arm extended eight and a half feet high, standing on tiptoe, I place my hand below a white handprint, bigger than my own large hand and for an instant, palm against shaded stone, I feel the same cold awe of the giants as they worshiped the cetacean Gods of the sea.

23

Fishy Government Business

Dolphin-style paddling—How a month in a kayak feels—
Bahía Concepción then and now—Trawling the sea—
PESCA: Mexico's joke

Roy Mayhoff and Becky Aparico are showing novice kayakers how to paddle on the banks of the Rio Mulegé. My shoulders are still sore so I listen carefully to Becky: "Dolphins use their spines to propel themselves, *effortlessly* through the water." She holds out a paddle and demonstrates with a quick-flowing, delphinoid grace. "By dipping one shoulder and twisting your torso, you use your spine and its twenty-five joints to pull you forward through the water—much more efficient than pumping with your arms and shoulders." If only we'd met Becky a month ago.

My shoulder grates like my knees do during a run. My rear end is so sore I can barely bend over. Deborah's technique is to lift her paddle high and push as if propelling a canoe—she has no pain. I have been using a pumpy, short-swing stroke to stop the grinding in my shoulder. Paddling hurts.

While resting in Mulegé, I spend time envisioning Becky's and Roy's "dolphin paddling," imagining the kayak as an extension of my back and legs. The last month has shown me how to savor the sensation of a kayak carving through the water, outdistancing black damselfish and yellow pompano, the water parting in front then closing behind cleaner than a ski wafting through powder snow.

Four decades ago a natural-history writer, Joseph Wood Krutch, came to Bahía Concepción (Becky's and Roy's base). He bumped along on a dirt track and saw prolific bird life, water that matched the sky, and a flaming flower not found in America. Krutch observed that the bay was one of the most immaculate places in the world. He drove along cliffed shorelines with his wheels kissing drop-offs and felt awed by the proliferation of sea life. Krutch wrote *The Forgotten Peninsula,* containing a chapter, "Seeing It the Hard Way." He observed that the cities of San Francisco and Oakland would easily fit in the uninhabited bay.

Bahía Concepción is now curbed by asphalt. Tourists see it the easy way, accessing hundreds of vacation homes, RV campsites, tourist shops, and kayaking schools—Mexigo, the National Outdoor Leadership School (NOLS), and Roy's and Becky's Bahía Tropicales.

Roy and Becky escort most kayaking clients several miles around the islets. They regularly encourage their novice charges to roll out of, rather than Eskimo-roll around in, their open-cockpit kayaks. They paddle up to the remains of boobie nests robbed bare by the locals. They snorkel ten feet down to butter clams and show clients how the bottom has been raked clean by clandestine shrimp trawlers or hundred-foot sardine boats, prohibited in the bay.

Three years ago, Roy says his kayaking clients had hundreds of birds surrounding them. Today Roy feels lucky if even a few birds follow his entourage. "Three years ago," Roy says, with hazel eyes flashing, "I saw big ole fish boils from our place at Santispac, but now feeding frenzies are a rare thing."

One night, Becky's and Roy's curiosity led them to ride with a Mexican shrimp trawler. Everything kicked up by the big wooden "gorilla" plank and caught in the purse net is dumped onto the deck in a ten-foot-by-four-foot pyramid of "writhing, squiggling, flopping sea life." Shrimp and squid constituted about 5 percent of the pile, while large rays, halibut, and an endangered tortoise (protected by law) were also culled out for the meat tender.

The crew finished culling out the edibles. Becky and Roy started pushing snakes, rays, sponges, small bottom fish, starfish, shellfish, and puffers overboard. The crew made them stop; if the creatures survived, they'd have to catch them all again, and reseparate them again from the edible fish. Becky and Roy watched, helpless and horrified, as the trawler raked the bay until morning, then dumped tons of dead "trash fish" in an area too deep for netting.

Since shrimp trawlers are only allowed to sell shrimp in the mainland port of Guaymas, illegally caught halibut, scallops, tortoise, puffer fish, mantas, and sea cucumbers are sold cheaply and on the sly in Mulegé—keeping trawling fishermen cashy and restaurateurs' refrigerators full. Recently, a restaurant in Mulegé celebrated its owner's fiftieth birthday by serving tortoise, attended, of course, by a PESCA official.

PESCA, the Federal Department of Fisheries, enforces fishing regulations. Roy has watched PESCA officials—paid thirty pesos (ten dollars) per day—enter Mulegé restaurants to check for improperly purchased fish. If there is no receipt from a legal fish market, the restaurateurs bribe PESCA officials thirty or forty pesos.

Roy, fifty-one years old, is pissed off. Here at the bar of the Serenidad Hotel he guzzles down a rum coke and pushes the condensation from the glass through his thinning hair. He describes boobies caught in fishing nets, the new Japanese demand for octopus, and the disappearance of scallops in the bay. Roy wants to be a crusader, but he feels more like an outsider fighting a battle that isn't his. "Nothing," he says, "is ever going to happen regardless of what we gringos do."

Mexicans are also pissed off. In February 1989, the Latin American environmentalists "Group of 100" wrote an open letter to President Salinas and protested PESCA corruption.

Last January, Mexican television presented a "60 Minutos" segment on how PESCA accepted 4.5 million dollars from Japanese for "fishing studies" in the Sea of Cortés, even though Salinas had supposedly shut down long-line fishing. And the monthly *Baja Sun* regularly runs front-page headlines about government fishing scandals. The August 1992 edition reads:

> Ecologists and sports fishing fleet owners are fighting the corruption with the fisheries department but the battle appears to be much like a dog chasing its own tail. Proof of illegal fishing and corruption with the department must be taken to . . . THE FEDERAL DEPARTMENT OF FISHERIES.

In Loreto, eighty-five miles south of Mulegé, a Mexican organization called Save the Sea of Cortés can't get the PESCA officials to come to its meetings. In Mulegé, several hundred locals signed a petition urging PESCA to enforce a fifty-mile fishing moratorium outside of Bahía Concepción; PESCA refused to come to the Mulegé Rotary meetings and receive the petition.

So one of Roy's Mexican friends went to them. He drove an hour north to Santa Rosalía during business hours and knocked on the PESCA office door, which was locked. In frustration, he walked to the Selena Cantina next door.

He found two guys swaying at the bar who'd been in there all day and when he asked them where he might find *los empleados* (slang for despised "little employees") from next door, the two PESCA officials meekly answered "aqui."

24

Day of the Dead

*Responsibility to the journey—Halloween in Mulegé—
Mexican philosophy of life—Smelling death—A strange cry
crossing Bahía Concepción*

All journeys must have context; all adventures must have isolation. Over the past month we have not isolated ourselves from
the people of the Sea of Cortés, who have taught us things we
would not have learned if we had avoided them. Yet we have
come south to be isolated from the "real world."

A family member might die, the house could burn down, a
career opportunity might wait on the answering machine, or a
forgotten bill could land in the mailbox. But life is too short.
Even a small imagination could conceive excuses that would
prevent anyone from going anywhere. Being responsible to the
journey is crucial. At the risk of being obdurate, an adventure
journey is a commitment of weighing anchor and not looking
back until the sail is finally trimmed.

Deborah and I sometimes see things differently.

In Mulegé, however, Deborah has a premonition that something is wrong and we agree that she can phone home as long as she does not give me any news. As Deborah walks to the phone booth, I sit on a cement-slab, wooden-back bench in the town plaza.

On Halloween, the eve of Mexico's two-day-long Día de los Muertos (Day of the Dead), gangs of face-painted and black-panted children rove the streets trick-or-treating. Día de los Muertos is one of the most important holidays in Mexico. Children accompany parents to cemeteries, clean tombstones, play special games, and offer gifts to their dead relatives.

Mexicans commune with the dead, not in the Christian sense of the hereafter so much as in the cultural belief that the past is not dead. Hence their constant reference to putting things off until "tomorrow" *(mañana),* and the inability, at PESCA or other government offices, for Mexicans to plan a future for themselves or their environment. Gringos commonly judge Mexicans as being indolent, but their culture is much more complex. They have a different concept of time; Mexicans tend to the past and let the fates shepherd the future.

I lounge on the cement bench contemplating the bustle of Halloween. Eight- and nine-year-old Vanessa and Mareta hold out a linen-wrapped basket and ask if I want some homemade bean empanadas. For once I am not hungry, so I tell the sisters that the empanadas smell delicious, and instead of exchanging money and goods, we talk. Once they become women they will not talk to American men.

They live a mile down the river. They intrigue me because they are more innocent and trusting than American children—as well as curious about me. They ask: "¿Dónde esta Colorado en Los Estados Unidos?"

"En las hermoso montañas," I reply. Vanessa and Mareta giggle at my kindergarten conjucating.

They take a picture of me with the camera, then I photograph them in their floral print dresses. Their knees are chalky with dirt and their black hair is pulled back on their heads to reveal wide cheekbones, inquisitive eyes, and impish smiles.

On the next bench two college professors lick ice cream cones and supervise their loose-leaf-notebook-clutching students as they run around town interviewing Mexicans. An old man approaches them, one foot in the grave, with sunken, black rings around his eyes setting off a blanched pallor. The academic man and woman of my own age recoil; the old man smiles, holds his head high with dignity, and says, "¡Buenos días!" The Americans neatly recover and talk around the man as if he is a ghost. He shuffles over to us. I seldom engage beggars, but this old man is different; he's dying. I ask Vanessa to introduce me. "Esta Frederico" she says and his back straightens up and a smile lifts the sagging sides of his pallid face. I shake his hand and tell him my name.

"Mucho gusto," he says quietly.

"No," I reply in Spanish, "the pleasure is all mine."

I give him some pesos and whisper, "Vaya con Díos."

Frederico nods his head and without any American beggar airs, he says, "Muchas gracias, Juan" and moves on.

Vanessa's and Mareta's mother appears with a furrowed brow—acknowledging me just as the Mexico 101 professors did Frederico—jerkily waving for the girls to get away from me.

Forty yards away, Deborah sobs uncontrollably into the phone and I know instantly, through the inexplicable radar that exists between husband and wife, that our dog Molly is dead.

We hold one another tightly and let tears wash our faces and time leaves us for a while because I do not know how we got back to the cement bench with the wooden back; it is too hard to stand, so we sit and bawl like children. I know Deborah feels guilty because if we didn't come to Mexico we could've been with Molly when she died of old age. Deborah thinks that Molly let go because we abandoned her—and it might be true.

Vanessa and Mareta reappear. The faces that were previously tight and unlined are now crinkled with consternation. I introduce them to Deborah, and they politely ask why we are crying.

"Porqué nuestros perro, Molly, es muerto," I answer, "y Molly esta neustros niña." They understand as best as children, or anyone for that matter, can understand. I explain that we loved our dog very much and that we are sad because Molly had a kind soul. They will not accept our sadness if only because they don't understand. They are children; they are Mexicans.

"Esta el Día de los Muertos," Mareta says. "Esta bien." The girls hug us and pass an empanada to lift some of the weight.

Even Deborah starts thinking Mexican. "When we get home," she says, "we'll have a big celebration for Molly."

Bahía Concepción broods with storm clouds. It's too rough to attempt the four-mile crossing, so we pull up onto the shore of a fishcamp with an abandoned shack. The tide is out and ghost crabs scuttle back into sable-brown sand holes. A booby tucks its wings, dives, pulls up at the last instant, and tucks again, skipping across the wave crests in two long bounces until it ducks its head to swallow a fish.

The shack smells sour. I put off going inside in order to see the shells out back—thousands of shells—shells burying some story. I climb up the conch hill, kick down one layer and there is a breaking pottery sound as I envision fishermen hammering the shells open, yanking out the meat, and throwing the empty conches out for years—until there are no more conches left in the sea. The fishermen leave.

Deborah stays outside of the shack and I hold my breath as I duck in under the doorway. Underneath a rickety plywood table is a bundle of black-matted fur and the fear-crossed eyes of a dead terrier. A nylon fishing rope is tied around its neck and deliberately half-hitched again around the leg of the table and my cheeks are suddenly wet again as I think of Molly and this dog and the conches outside. There is a connection here,

something about our unbearable inhumanity to all creatures great and small. Then I make the mistake of breathing in too deeply and I rush out into fresh air, weak kneed and ready to faint. *Welcome to Mexico, honey,* I think.

"Deb," I say, "Don't bother going in."

"Why not?"

"Just don't because it really reeks in there."

Halfway across, the sea has calmed. The sky is as rich as an algae bloom. Deborah is several hundred yards back, as currents deflect her lighter boat during crossings. I stop to dip my hands in the water, as if I might feel what is coming out of the barren Bahía Concepción. The water is cold, clear, dark. Obsessing like an old poker player, I can't read what's under the deck. A distant wailing comes over the water—the cry of some recognizable bird. I put down my paddle. The sound carries to me again on the wind, loud and unmistakable, and I realize it's Deborah crying.

25

Killer Whale
in Repose

*Creating a sea—Schools of kayakers—A coyote, vultures,
and a whale—Nature's graveyard*

Paddling eighty-five miles from Mulegé to Loreto is the most
popular of all Baja California kayak tours. Although sandy
beaches aren't as frequent as those up north, between Mulegé
and Loreto there are islands, few access roads, insignificant
tides, and minor currents. Unlike the northern section, deepen-
ing waters and a widening sea reduce tidal pull and current.
Still, it's no bathtub during storms.

During the Pliocene period 5 million years ago, Baja California
was attached to mainland Mexico. As the Pacific tectonic plates

gradually shifted away from the North American plates, an eight-hundred-mile chunk of mainland was pulled off and stretched like taffy 125 miles northwest, dropping off small gobs of islands and creating a sea (of Cortés) that reached as far as Palm Springs. Volcanic activity seared this peninsular piece of taffy, and volcanoes bubbled up, on land and sea (Islas Raza, San Luis, and Smith—to name a few). It took millions more years for the Colorado River to fill the northern sea with sediment.

So the Colorado River got plugged and the Tourism Epoch began. Mulegé, Loreto, Bahía Concepción, Isla Espirítu Santo, Bahía Los Angeles, and Bahía Magdalena became burgeoning, sea-kayaking destinations. During our week's paddle to Loreto, we'll see twenty-two Japanese guided by Baja Expeditions, three NOLS groups of fifteen to nineteen people, three men from Alta California, two Coloradans, and another married couple. North of Mulegé, we saw only three kayakers.

South of Mulegé we overtake two Colorado taxi drivers. Andy and Skip are admittedly ill-prepared, having rented two open-cockpit kayaks—more intended for bay snorkeling than coastal expeditions. They are towing a third inflatable kayak with camping gear. Deborah voluntarily clips its towrope onto her rear deck to help them and because one of her métiers in life is competing with men. Paddling for an hour without the monkey on their backs, Andy and Skip talk openly. The twenty-nine-year-old Skip owns a successful taxi company in Telluride. He says that the money means nothing to him and he wants to sell out and spend his life on more meaningful pursuits like paddling the Sea of Cortés.

Deborah gradually cedes to my impatience at the slowed pace. We say good-bye, she relinquishes their inflatable kayak, and we cross a churning bay, hoping to round the next point before the wind picks up. Without her payload, Deborah's acceleration reminds me of the space-bound Apollo space capsule jettisoning its empty bottom booster. Keeping up with my wife is work; my shoulder sounds like a crackling bowl of Rice

Krispies every time I push the paddle. I think of a dolphin wiggling through the water and how responsive my kayak has become. My feet no longer cramp against the rudder pedals and I turn the boat by tensing my hips against the gunwales, leaning into big swells without conscious thought and power paddling out the opposite side, laughing at the "snap crackle pop" of my shoulder joint. The spare tire that rode my waist a month ago is now washboarded roadbed. Deborah's body is greyhoundish curves—graceful muscles and thick blue veins tracing her arms like road maps.

We pass the first NOLS group, spread out over a beach where we had hoped to camp. Rather than stopping, we opt to round one more point, practicing good etiquette by leaving them alone. An hour later, we pull our spray skirts on in bouncing water. As we paddle into the refuge of a bay, yet another group of ten NOLS kayaks and tarps are spread out across the beach. We paddle in to the side, to a cobbled beach, so that we won't interrupt NOLS. The landing is tricky: surfing onto rocks, pulling off our spray skirts and dashing out before the sea can slam our hulls against rocks.

Fifteen students watch an instructor paddle out into their sheltered bay. Another instructor intercepts us at shouting distance so that we won't disrupt their capsize class. She is bearishly thick-boned, as formidable as a linebacker, glancing with admiration at Deborah's lean, mean musculature—pride flushes over me. The instructor explains that the students in her group, as well as the other two NOLS groups nearby, are all ravaged by dysentery, spread like a wildfire by their shared cooking pots.

NOLS instructors are superb teachers, but nineteen people subverts the "minimum impact" goal of wilderness travel. No matter how diligent a large group is, their abandoned campsites will hide feces, campfire ashes, trash, and trampled flora—not found in smaller groups' campsites. Groups the size of Skip's and Andy's (whom the NOLS instructors openly snubbed for their unpreparedness while passing them the previous day), have the pleasure of learning the hard way—from their mistakes—without an instructor setting schedules.

Deborah and I discuss rounding the next point. The bear-ish instructor frowns about the wisdom of paddling such bumpy water—they sat out the last day waiting for growing cloud, wind, and diarrhea storms to subside—but we aren't in-vited to share the only good beach.

Thunder growls out over the sea and as our bows slam into wave troughs we respond by leaning forward and timing our paddle strokes. We call it quits just as the water starts com-ing in over our spray skirts. We pitch our tent next to an arroyo studded with tires, fishing nets, and nonbiodegradable bottles.

"Plastic," Deborah says as we walk south, "godawful, ubiq-uitous plastic."

Two miles from camp, a coyote bounds away from the ocean; a smell of sour fat rides the wind. Distant vultures hold fingertipped wings up in a 110-degree dihedral from their bel-lies—distinguishing them from raptors' right-angled wing posi-tioning.

A ten-foot-long killer whale lies on the shore below. We walk closer. Its black skin is rotted gray, its belly pulses with surf. I run a finger, tentatively, across thick, inch-high teeth: sharp yel-low cutting tools; I pull my hand back. An eye is missing and in the empty socket a sheer membrane breathes with the surf. Blue, gas-ballooned intestines bulge out of a hole on its side.

Why the long-dead killer whale has not yet been eaten by predators is puzzling. The normally avaricious vultures are holding back, as if the whale, even in death, still swims atop the food chain.

One of our partners from Denali, Rick Ridgeway, told us about killer whales beside Isla Tiburón. Early one morning, on a half-mile-long cliff, Rick went solo climbing; falling seemed of minor consequence because he would've simply jumped forty feet down into the sea. An osprey circled above, crying shrilly, and down in the calm sea below Rick a whale spouted water mixed with carbon dioxide; the handholds were small and Rick was startled by his closeness to the big whales. Two of them stopped, while the third charged a rock ledge just beside Rick. The killer whale shimmied up out of the water, cocking its head looking for sea lions as its partners waited out in the water for fleeing prey, but the ledge was uninhabited.

As the killer whales continued hunting, Rick crawled into a cave, his "synapses on full fight-or-flight predator alert." Rick knows that whales aren't supposed to prey upon humans, but as he crouched in the cave, trembling, he wondered what the killer whales would do if he fell into the sea.

In Bahía Los Angeles, Pepé Smith told me about guiding a whale biologist around the bay in a *panga*. Pepé says a killer whale chased them for ten minutes with its mouth wide open (he demonstrated, staggering and pouring in some of his Tecate), as Pepé held the *panga* throttle wide open, "staying just ten feet in front of the killer whale's jaws until I drove the *panga* up onto a beach and we ran away." It sounded like a fish story until I pressed him; he admitted: "Maybe I started it all by motoring too close to its calf."

The killer whale—speciously referred to by part of its Latin name *orca*—resembles a wolf by its reasoning, communication, and social proclivities. Scientists once watched fifteen killer whales in the northern sea chasing a Bryde's whale until it became too exhausted to flee. Then the killer whales took turns swimming atop their prey's forty-foot-long back—preventing it from surfacing—effectively drowning the Bryde's whale.

The subadult in front of us may have died during such a campaign (or in a fishing net) and floated for days as its mother fended off sharks; the carcass beached and it could no longer be protected. On the shoreline above the dead whale are a myriad of flowers: a sweet-smelling pink flower growing on blood-colored vines, yellow shrublike spurges—related to the poinsettia—and a purple, sharply foul-smelling member of the daisy family. Pitaya cacti are blowing their crimson trumpet flowers up on the hillsides.

The misting rain explains the teem of flowers and it occurs to us that a killer whale could not find a more apropros resting place. Here at the edge of the sea—fertilizing the spurges, carried over the cacti in vulture craws, picked upon by sally lightfoot crabs, and filling coyote bellies—the whale will disappear more cleanly than bones in a graveyard. Its remains will evaporate into the foaming blue littoral as naturally as clouds seeding the desert.

26

⤛ ❧ ⤜

What Purpose
Do We Serve?

*A seven-Motrin day—Life and Death—The Dancing
Needlefish—Night surfing*

Since the tides are gentler in this southerly section of sea, big
boats often appear. A cruiser as long as a tandem semi passes
us out at sea and we forget it until four, five-foot swells arrive,
swirling white on their tops, threatening to swamp us; we kick
our rudder pedals and paddle into the wake.

Deborah and I gauge the pleasure of each day's paddling
by designating it a "one" through "ten"—how many Motrin
anti-inflammatory pills, or vitamin M, we eat ("a ten-Motrin
day" means we're hurting; one Motrin or none means, as they
say, that we're having "a nice day"). We pull into a protected
sandy cove, weary of the noontime winds. It is only a three-

Motrin day, but I feel ragged: my head aches from lack of water and too much sun, while my shoulder feels as if the surgical screw is ready to pop. As Deborah reads, I stretch out beside what little shade my knee-high boot offers, prop my head on an arm, and fall asleep as wind whistles through the mast. No dreams come.

As I open my eyes sometime later, my head moves on my neck like a storm door-hinge opening in thirty below. I come awake seeing the world anew, wondering why I am here, wondering what purpose I serve.

Sanderlings sprint through the tidal estuary, forced to race against their insatiable metabolism for a half-dozen years until dead. Vibrant green beach-grass shoots skyward, as if to refute this forsaken piece of desert shore. I flatten a mosquito on my arm so it can't breed legions more. Stingrays spring out of the sea like so much flung pizza dough. Vultures pick over a pile of fly-blown triggerfish carcasses, as misplaced as vulture bones on an underwater reef. Life sometimes seems so full of hard ironies and unanswerable questions. Life has so much *weight* that I wonder if these creatures, on their own levels—through intelligent cognition or electrical impulses or nerve synapses or brain waves—also wonder what purpose they serve.

I once knew a Native American who shouldered this same weight, but rather than admit it, Ted always posed the question as if it applied only to others. When Nellie left him, he asked, "Heyyyy, what purpose did she serve?" When his son committed suicide, he asked, "Heyyy, what purpose did he serve?" He took his retirement pension and moved into a cabin in the thick forest and grappled with the question quietly on his own through his long winters of night, until loneliness drove him to an abyss and finally, a massive heart attack gripped his chest. I wonder if he lay there dying in the dark forest asking himself: "What purpose do I serve?"

I eat four more vitamin M and what started as merely a three-Motrin day is becoming a hurting day. In the hopes of salvaging something, I yank out the repair kit and begin patch-ing the scraped-up kayak hull. In places, only a single layer of transparent fiberglass separates my rear end from the sea. I goop on a half pound of epoxy and two pieces of thick fiberglass cloth. My fingers are white with epoxy, but repair jobs always put me back on my feet.

In a chest-high forest of sour *dulce* pitaya cacti, all of the tomato-sized fruit has been sucked dry by cactus wrens or insects. Our limited food compels us, like former Cochimi, to gather something—anything. So at high tide, I stand on the wave-battered Punta Colorado, casting again and again into a seemingly barren sea while Deborah writes in her journal beyond surf range. From nowhere, an unexpected wave blasts me off my perch and sends me sputtering into the sea; I keep the fishing rod only because the lure accidentally catches my shorts. As I scramble out, scraping my arms and hands raw on coral before the next wave can suck me back in, Deborah is oblivious: her face buried in her hands as she weeps about our Molly. If there is nothing else in life, if the sea is dead, at least we can turn to one another. Maybe *this* is the purpose we serve: loving one another. I rush over for mutual first aid.

We never spend time on a mountain or a sea without studying its history because we want to know in what particular places we need to pay attention. As we paddle out around Punta Santa Theresa we are nervous about the violence with which the water slaps against our hulls and splashes in our faces, and the sea's radical bend around the peninsula. We are nervous because it is here that the nine Outward Bound students clung to their kayaks all night long until three let go and died.

We resume a new southeasterly course and the waters calm as suddenly as shutting a faucet on a filled bathtub. Fish are jumping into the sky and birds are diving into the water in a splashing tryst of role reversal. I release the bail on my rod strapped to the gunwale, count to five to let out line, then flip the bail shut to stop the lure's plunge.

No sportshop salesperson would ever recommend such a thin rod for ocean fishing. The inner gears of my old lake-fishing reel are rusted and stripped—saved only by a daily oiling and cleaning dissembly. Someone suggested using a flyrod, but purchasing and learning how to cast a flyrod would subvert my philosophy of fishing to eat. I have no interest in playing with fish, then releasing them by tearing the hooks out of their mouths, all under the guise of being "a sportsman." With this rod, if the fish is too big it gets away; if it's the right size for dinner, I reel it in.

Flying fish and jumping needlefish splash on either side of our boats. The needlefish is my favorite fish partly because it is not considered good eating, even though it has sweet and tender meat, and partly because it is so hard to catch—barracuda-sharp teeth and aerial acrobatics cut monofilament lines like hot knives on rime; so I have tied my lure onto a sixteen-inch-long steel leader.

A needlefish, *Tylosurus crocodilus,* nails the lure behind me like a cat on a mouse and begins dancing on the water forty yards back. I spin the rod tip skyward and shout for Deborah's help. Line zings out my reel so I let the needlefish dash toward the Mexican mainland until it leaps out of the water curling into a three-foot circumference, letting me reel in another ten yards, as I lean shoreward to stay afloat. Deborah steadies my boat by catamaraning us together. The sea is splashing rough again.

The needlefish continues jumping, writhing, arcing, shaking, and shooting straight out of the water in an attempt to shed the lure. My only chance is to be patient and bring the fish in by gently flexing the rod back—the cogs are so stripped it only reels in if the line is slack. I coerce the fish to the boat, and it swims out and around us, whizzing the nylon filament against the water and into our rudders, nearly breaking the line.

After two more runs and a half hour's fencing, it relents. The needlefish comes alongside my boat gasping, yawning dozens of teeth up and down like studded needlenose pliers. Deborah excuses herself as I sever its spine in the water with a quick crunching plunge of the knife, then lash quarter-inch polypropylene through its gills and mouth onto the rear deck.

The sky's popsicle-orange afterglow fades and landing prospects are poor. While checking out a rocky cove between wave sets, I misjudge the water's depth and am suddenly confronted by a set of three seven-foot waves. Fortunately, Deborah is on the seaward side of the reef, shouting about my pending capsize. I paddle with bowed head and submarine through the first cresting wave, then paddle hard into the second wave, which lifts my bow sixty degrees as I throw my weight forward and the wave releases me in its rear trough with a bone-jarring splash. Still upright, scared that the third and biggest wave will equal an ocean yard sale of kayaking gear, I brace my paddle as the wave breaks in my face, rips off the spray skirt, and fills the boat with gallons of seawater before launching me behind the wave, slamming me down, miraculously upright, nimble as a six-hundred-pound needlefish.

Deborah and I are mute with disbelief. I should have swam.

The sky is dark except for a narrow strip of vermilion to the east; the sea and air are ebony walls. Without a safe beach, we will have to paddle all night, because surfing onto rocks will trash kayaks and kayakers. We paddle south. I ask Deborah: "Can you keep going?"

She accuses me of spending too much time fishing, which accounts for our present troubles.

Instead of acknowledging my mistake, I console her: "It'll be okay. Let's listen for the surf sound to change from hitting rocks to hitting sand."

"Yeah, like we're gonna be able to tell!" she shouts.

Some Mexican fishermen hear us out in the water and hold up a lantern, silently signaling their safe beach. I listen for the breaking line of waves, paddle to its edge, and wait for a set to pass before rushing the shore. On the slack water I paddle all out, as fast as my arms and back and stomach can carry me; faster than the water, fast as a dolphin. Sixty yards from shore another wave catches me and lifts my kayak into the air until the boat feels as if it's flying atop a carpet of aerated water so I lean back and listen to the bow sensuously cutting water and bay heretically to the night (and five astonished Mexicans): "GODDDDDDDDDDDDDDAMN!!!" The wave lifts the boat all the way up to high-tide line and I jump out, my bloodless legs crashing me face flat against sand.

I shout two hundred yards out to Deborah: "You're gonna love it!"

Minutes later, she appears on the beach as a yellow blur of whooping kayak, leaning backward like a stuck aerobics instructor, and promptly tripping as she exits the boat. No matter. We're safe.

We pull the boats up higher than we can imagine a storm tide. I hug her; she pushes me off because she's still scared; my fingers are jiggling with adrenaline.

Then we pause to admire *Tylosurus crocodilus*, staring with limpid and fixed eyes, strung between my flippers and emergency throwline like a muscular length of toothed pipe. Deborah refuses to eat it. I will relish every bite for two days. It glints silvery green against the surrounding cloak of night, and it has such unlikely form. *Tonight this acrobat showed me how to dance above the waters*, I think, *and the best I can do is show my respect by eating it.*

27

Bugs

*Illusion of a manta—Kayak surf lesson—All creatures pretty and small—*Pescador *gentleman*

Stingrays and manta rays vault. Rock pedestals are mounted with pelicans and frigatebirds, preening with crooked beaks, cooing for the returning tide. One ray jumps so high that it is framed against a cloud on the horizon, flapping its wings and holding air for a scant second until it plummets, more rock than bird. A large turtle with a sad, downturned mouth surfaces near Deborah again and again, with curious blinking eyes, until it finally sounds and departs.

Spring pelicans watch as the adults dive for fish. Belted kingfishers' rattles are amplified tenfold from a cave. A Costa hummingbird whirrs out to us in a blur of green, white, and purple gorget, circling us, and once satisfied Deborah's yellow kayak is not a damiana flower, returns to shore.

The closest most gringos come to identifying the flower is

by its female-body-shaped bottles in liquor stores. *Bajacali-fornios* know damiana as an aromatic, five-petaled flower, commonly sold as dried green leaves in Mexican apothecaries. *Bajacalifornios* say that drinking damiana tea improves your sex life; gringos pour the liquor in margaritas to reach the same net result.

Astride a breaking wave, my bow submarines into the still water and I lean back to balance my watery sea-saw but the whole boat slides in front of the wave onto still water and turns sideways. This is unexpected, but my reactions are common sense: lean to port and brace the paddle up like a canoe paddle to prevent tipping, then surf sideways to shore. Deborah surfs in, *straight* in, while rain pocks the smooth water behind her.

Fine, pasty brown sand sticks to our skin. Beach grass grows out of donkey shit; rabbit pellets pebble the sand. Invisible *jejénes* bite our wrists and the webbing between our toes.

After a two-inch-long scorpion scuttles under my boat, lobstering its stinger tail aloft, Deborah pulls the nylon cover over her kayak cockpit—mainland Mexico scorpions contain deadly neurotoxic venom. Here on the peninsula, there is only one person known to have died from a scorpion sting, packing the wallop of a wasp. Ammonia (or urine) rubbed on the wound neutralizes the venom's toxic proteins. So we dive in our tent, pull our shoes inside, zip the net door firmly shut, and sweat like sauna dwellers. Even the rain's cessation can't persuade us to sleep outside.

With his unerring naturalist eye, Father Baegert may have been the first to call scorpions "pretty little animals." After being bitten, he reported that the bite only causes swelling and pain for several hours. "The color of the California scorpion is yellow-green," he wrote, "and some are as long as a finger, not counting the tail."

No place on earth hosts as many as Baja California's sixty-one scorpion species. The western United States has fifty-eight

species, Italy has five, and Florida has four. Biologists have found the greatest diversity of scorpions—thirteen different species—right here in mid-lower peninsula, rather than up north. (Deborah asks me to go out and fetch something from her boat and I refuse.)

Dinnertime gurgles with gastric anticipation in our stomachs. We unzip the tent and dash out as if avoiding sniper fire, out to the water line, where a breeze discourages the similarly hungry *jejénes*.

I dissemble the plugged-up stove upon a nylon bag and blow out the sticky grains of sand, soak it for ten minutes in gas, then wipe the orifice and burner assembly clean with my tee shirt. It starts anew, roaring like a *panga*—so when a *panga* pulls out from a nearby cove, we don't hear it. Deborah is naked as a Cochimi at the water's edge, cleaning sand out of her bathing suit, and the fisherman, after only glancing our way, averts his head and holds his eyes out to sea, long enough for Deborah to dress.

Deborah picks out the sweet, albacore-tender chunks of needlefish from her fish taco and passes them to me. Something about its soft texture, something about watching me gut it, prevents Deborah from eating any needlefish. Moths fly around our faces, into our mouths, and onto our food. Crabs scuttle back and forth amid incoming waves, plucking at their own microbial food.

Golden-and-black-striped poliste wasps alight on us and our dinner. We shoo them away and they come back, floating in like cottonwood seeds, brandishing their stingers and working their pinchers above our skin—I can tolerate them no longer. They are as stunning as scorpions, but admiring them at the risk of being stung is nerve-racking. "Man always kills the things he loves," Aldo Leopold wrote about the Colorado River delta, "and so we the pioneers have killed the wilderness." I swat twenty-three dead.

A praying mantis the size of my index finger flies out of the dunes and lands on my foot, cleaning its two antennae by raking them with a green palpus. Rock lice see it and scatter down the beach; even the moths leave. Then the praying mantis stops preening, looks at me with unusually large eyes, and twists its head like a curious dog. I shoo it off.

Back in the tent, sheltered from the bugs, I rub Deborah's sore neck. *Jejénes* cover the outside of the netting in a fine black mist. I double-check that the door zipper is shut tight.

Eventually, the rhythmic sweep of sea against shore lulls us asleep on top of our sleeping bag, covered with filmy sweat and sand. In the dark of night the roaring comes and I jump from my dreams, screaming, "NO, NO!" zip open the door, and peer up into the blackness for the tsunami: it is a jet in landing pattern for Loreto.

The tent fills with hungry *jejénes.*

28

Mahi-mahi

*Sand cleaning—Fish stories—Making words and defining
our relationship—Night paddling*

Before we can paddle, the beach has to be separated from
gear. We dunk tent, stuff sacks, dry bags, sleeping pads, sleeping bag, and tee shirts repeatedly into the sea, but the sand
clings like glue. I dive into a wave and shake underwater. Pushing the water through my hair, I then use my fingernails to
scrub age-old turtle shell, sharks' teeth, conches, whalebone,
oysters, fish scales, and clams—mixed with peninsular
bedrock—off my body.

An hour later, we're still spitting sand from our teeth.
frigatebirds swoop down on feeding gulls; I put down the paddle and circle my fingers in both ears to dab out annoying
grains.

A big dolphinfish, the first we've seen, plunks up out of
the water, chasing prey across our bows. Its big sail fin hums

against the wind during four jumps, flashing by in a blur of green and blue.

Catching a twenty- to seventy-pound dolphinfish—also known as dorado or *mahi-mahi*—let alone holding it on my tackle, would be akin to Ahab taking Moby Dick with a harpoon. Besides, it's too much fish for us to keep without the meat spoiling. Judging by Ray Cannon's "white whalish" summations in his *Sea of Cortez* book, fishing for dorado from a kayak is a long shot—most dorado are caught from trolling powerboats, hitting the bait while traveling in opposite directions, as fast at forty miles per hour.

Cannon wrote:

> If asked what was the most enthralling thing I have ever seen in the Cortez . . . I would select the time I saw a school of about a hundred dolphin fish rainbowing up in unison for a fifty-foot-long leap. . . .
>
> There seems to be no satisfying the ravenous appetite of the dolphin fish. I have seen them snatch baits just a few inches in front of the noses of big sharks and billfish. At first sight of a tobogganing bait, this voracious creature, like the needlefish, often takes off from a great distance and comes bounding through the air, or rips up the surface for a hundred yards to be first at a morsel. When hooked, it bounds as high as fifteen feet. I know of no other fifty- to seventy-five-pound swimmer that . . . keep[s] the fishing rod in the shape of a question mark for an hour and a half.
>
> Add to this all the hocus-pocus tricks the protean showoff uses to flamboozle a fisherman: a hundred-yard peel-off straight away, then a sudden reversal right toward the boat; quick, unexpected slips under the craft, across its bow, then under and up near the outboard prop. . . . Finally, if all else fails to dislodge the hook, the creature will possum until the over-

confident angler relaxes the line, then spit the hook out right in front of the premature victor.

Cannon's fishing fables hooked the imaginations of count-less gringo fishermen. Loreto became a destination for dolphin-fish expeditions. *Sports Illustrated, Outdoor Life,* and *Western Outdoor News* all hyped the dorado fishing until the late 1980s, when old hands finally lamented that *El Niño,* and not overfish-ing, had removed most of the dorado.

My shoulder is still tender. As I dip the paddle to water, ever so gently, I make words and sentences to pass the time, to ease the strain. As I haul my kayak up stones clicking with surf, I am thinking about the words for my journal, instead of my kayak; a twenty-gallon wave washes over the stern and steals my seat.

I turn to my journal:

So sore i can't bend over. "Am i getting old?" i asked Deb. She was so supportive as i griped and pulled over to fix seat, readjust pedals. Finally sitting on life jacket fixed falling-asleep legs (sore butt). 10 Motrin day. Paddling like a dolphin alleviated grinding in my R shoulder. Not so fast a stroke and i repeatedly re-quested Deb to slow down. It's hardest when she paddles ahead, stops, waits, paddles ahead, stops, waits, etc. It's hard because i take security in knowing i'm strong. Have to readjust—that's what this trip is about in so many ways: accommodating and support-ing one another's strengths and weaknesses. i surely don't want Deb, my wife no less, to feel as if she can't out do me physically. We're so goddamned competi-tive with each other.

Why did we come? Really? Because so much of my life—peoples' lives—are about fleeing. By coming

here, i want to confront the basis of our union together. i want to give *real* wings to our marriage and
make it explode up out of the water and into the very
sky that defies the mantas.

Sea splashes warm on my hands. This dark window of water, lit
by the syrupy glow of the waxing moon, harbors an unearthly
danger—ready-wound for some ancient leathery-skinned creature to spring from the depths and shatter the stillness with a
thrashing of fins and clacking of teeth against fiberglass. I feel
like a child under the bed in darkness. Deborah can read me
better than I read my own watch: she's humming that ominous
bass tune from the movie *Jaws;* I wonder if loving her is related
to never being cut any slack. But I probably deserve it.

Where is the sun? I recheck my watch and it still reads 6
A.M. but I am reading the alarm mode instead of the time mode;
the time reads 3:09 A.M. So I confess to Deborah, but she
doesn't mind because she likes the strange novelty of night
paddling.

The shore could be a mile or even short yards away. I paddle close enough to keep the surf's gentle breath in my right
ear. A wave rolls my kayak onto the shore and I push off the
sand with my palms and paddle back out. Deprived of vision, I
scrounge for sensory input, repeatedly taking the temperature
of the water with my fingers; sniffing the briny air as if some
message might lie beyond the moonlight; flinching when a fish
splashes behind me. My life flashes like a movie screen in front
of me, filling the void left by the darkness: after the great white
shark of my imagination departs, I see our dog: nose dry, hob-
bling and crying with arthritis. It comes clearer than the sunrise
that Molly's death is bringing Deborah and me closer. With
Molly gone, Deborah and I only have one another.

I am shaking, prickly-skinned. I have to get off this cold
sea—I know it's mostly galloping emotions and nighttime illu-

sions, but above the untold, graveyard depths of this sea, I can no longer confront my fears. I suggest to Deborah that the current might be carrying us out, and she immediately reads the paranoia in my voice. I don't have to give it words. We pull in on the outskirts of Loreto, sprawl out on the sand, and lie in the warmth of one another's arms waiting for the sun.

29

After the Jesuits

Journey of the Flame—*Burp and you die*—*Last of the*
Cochimi—*End of civilization*—*The ironies of modern Loreto*

In 1809, a redheaded mestizo, Juan Obrigón, walked fifteen hundred miles from San José to San Francisco to see what remained in his country after the Jesuits. Although the Vermilion Sea was still pristine, he and his companions wanted to visit the last of the Indian tribes, just as we are visiting the sea.

In his biography, *Journey of the Flame,* Obrigón has a wry voice. The Jesuits " . . . felt God had called them to save the souls of millions of Indians, who did not know they had souls, and always politely resented having souls forced upon them."

Obrigón was born near San José. He was sired by an Irish sailor who jumped ship, slept with Obrigón's fair-skinned, mestizo mother, and promptly abandoned Baja California.

Eleven years later, the precocious redhead walked north on a trail painstakingly cut by Indians and soldiers (its cobbled remnants are clearly seen from the sea, snaking across cliffs, rutted into clay banks). This "Royal Highway" connected Loreto's mission, north and south, with all the mission pueblos on the peninsula. A 1730 Spanish walker wrote "In opening trails . . . more labor has been expended in California in thirty-four years than in the whole of New Spain from the beginning of the Conquest through two centuries."

This trail became the narrative thread for Obrigón's tales, just as the Sea of Cortés defines our own journey. From the trail, Obrigón describes the Indians outside of Loreto:

> There came to me . . . an Indian who whispered to me in his own language, "One of your men just hic-coughed [burped]," and while I struggled not to laugh, for this is a deadly offense, and stops all flow of information from the natives, he repeated, "He hic-coughed."
>
> "He has eaten too much," I answered, for the man he spoke of was a gross feeder.
>
> "It is not 'The disease' then?" he questioned, much relieved.

Father Baegert wrote about Indians with "erudications of such violent character that the noise almost resembled thunder, and could be heard at a distance of forty and more paces." The burps (dysentery attacks) lasted several minutes and eventually killed the Indians. Obrigón's Spanish biographer, Antonio Blanco, wrote: "In truth, these natives were not without reason in their fears, since they had no resistance to those infections we Spaniards felt only slightly. . . . [N]o one knows why Indians die so easily."

In Loreto, Obrigón vaunts about "the best mandarin oranges in the world," as well as olives and pearls. He describes missionary crops being ravaged by millions of locusts—a mysterious scourge that vanished, Obrigón claims, after the Jesuits left. He describes Indians starving to death as the Franciscans (replacing the Jesuits) rode north with food-larded saddlebags, refusing to feed the heathens. And he describes Spain's prohibition on growing crops, "lest Spanish commerce be injured, though thereby every man in California was taught to hate Spain."

Obrigón reveals that the Spaniards started North America's first boarding school for girls in Loreto in 1771, housing six hundred Indians. The girls were taught to cook, clean house, and wear clothing. A few years later, the school inexplicably closed and the girls "were turned loose to live without clothes, eat bugs, and dwell in the open without roof through summer and winter."

Obrigón counted five hundred books in the Loreto library "but 400 souls in Loreto" and only a handful of citizens could read. Obrigón was illiterate, yet guessed the books' contents from pictures of "Saints expiring in various cruel ways such as our Indians would be ashamed to practice."

And of the "richly decorated" Loreto church, he could only surmise that the square was cobbled because hogs would not sleep on stones, and Salvatierra, the mission's founder, would not have to kick them away while walking to mass.

The beginning of the nineteenth century, Obrigón says, was an era when "human life was not of great value." With his Indian, Spanish, and Irish blood, Obrigón was the first Mexican writer to evaluate the remains of his beloved peninsula. After the last of the Indians had died from various diseases, eighty years after Obrigón's journey, his biographer concluded that "civilization speaks for itself in Lower California."

In Loreto, we trip and toil under nine grocery bags. The volume of Mexican music from passing cars shakes windows and rattles palm fronds. Loudspeakers on the roof of a battered Pinto endorse a new electoral candidate so loudly that we drop the bags and hold hands over our ears as it passes; people in street-side houses defend themselves by cranking up the volumes of their televisions.

The first mission in Baja California, founded 296 years ago by Salvatierra, was rebuilt in 1704 on its present site. After a *chubasco* razed most of Loreto in 1829, sparing the church, the capitol was moved to La Paz. The church's square has been re-cobbled, although the boxy shape appears more jailhouse than church. A clock has been added to the highest turret. The antiqued church bell's pealing, with no correlation to the clock or any religious event, almost drowns out the Pinto—prowling down the next street.

In the same square where Father Salvatierra preached to the heathens—condemning pitaya revelries and wanton behavior—Loreto teens are sucking cherry Popsicles and shouting come-ons to would-be mates across the church plaza.

30

Verdancy

Our rattling relationship—Reveling in rain—Fulfillment—
Letting the land imprint me—Sitting below sea level

Paddling out of Loreto, Deborah chides me: "Don't you think I
know that the weather is bad and you don't have to warn me?"
I apologize and tell her I'm just talking aloud. She remains on
the defensive all morning. *How many years have men and*
women walked the earth, I think, *and we're still trying to figure*
out how to talk with one another? After a few miles under scud-
ding black clouds and angry seas, we stop and pitch the tent.
She picks up a book; I make words in my journal:

> i consider it nothing shy of a miracle that we're still
> together. Perhaps the stress inherent in this sort of trip
> is too much for us. Sometimes in potential diff/dan-
> ger, she becomes shrill, contrary, even panicky; then
> again, i just clam up entirely.

i told her i loved her more than i've ever loved anyone. Her reply: "Who did you love before?"

Sometimes i wonder if loving someone is defined by
once in a while stooping to detesting that someone.
i'll have to ask if she does the same thing but i already
know the answer.

Dime-sized raindrops calm the briny sea. We steer toward
Isla Danzante, named after dancing Indians who greeted the
seventeenth-century pearler, Francisco de Ortega. As the rain
relents, the sea begins swaying. Low black clouds drape the
towering green peaks of the mainland like layers of floating
Spanish moss.

As the raindrops plunk down again, the sea goes black
and flat as a hammered anvil. I pull on a raincoat. I pull it off
once I start sweating, then tilt back to catch fat raindrops in my
mouth. A brown mantle of clouds buries the sun. Isla Danzante
and Isla Carmen poke up out of the sea, sunburned red, re-
minding us what it was like before the rain came.

It rains and rains and rains. We paddle contentedly in be-
calmed waters because, for once, the rain cools us and adds a
mystical dimension: making the island peaks look other-
worldly, as high as the reddened peaks of Mars, giving us the
sensation that we're paddling on a sea of clouds. At night we
avoid flash-flooding canyons and catch the sweet rainwater in
cups and pots positioned beneath corners of the tent. The
peninsula swells greenly, dotted with flowers, fringing the face
of the sea as a vast fur ruff.

I find a white, long-legged spider stranded upon the bow
of my kayak. I paddle back to our former campsite, cradle the
spider in my hand, then jump out and release it beneath a gos-
samer strand, holding up a fishhook cactus like a guyline.

The rain allows us to paddle two feet away from normally
turbulent cliffs, drifting past sleeping sea lions and over a rainbow of colorful fish skittering through the reefs.

The rain enriches us. The last six weeks have made us feel as parched as the deserts we have passed, but as the rain whisks against the tent walls by night, dappling the water by day, I feel sated, a vessel that can only be filled by Baja California. By sea and desert. Love and detestation. Culture and wilderness. Joy and fear. Clouds and stars. Sunshine and rain.

Finally, on November 8, the sky clears for the first time in weeks. Fishermen out at sea ply nets from their *pangas,* their lower bodies obfuscated by the movement of hot air and wave sets as if they are standing upon water.

We pull into a small protected bay ten miles south of Punta Candeleros. For some reason the beaches are cleaner than those north of the midriff. I stroll past burned pieces of driftwood, bleached and spineless urchin shells, a Maxwell House jar (with the lid on), foot-long lobster carapaces and legs, the top to an oilcan, a sandal, a Negro Modela can, purplish-green seaweed, oyster shells, rope, another lidded glass jar, and cow pies.

A riot of yellow butterflies wafts down from a cliff and passes over like a saffron cloud. Fresh coyote tracks pepper the littoral. Dozens of inch-deep holes, lined with webbing, crater the sand—a wolf spider waits nearby for an insect to stumble in.

Deborah picks up a two-inch fiddler crab and, looking eye to eye, Homo sapiens and crustacean stare into one another's white and stalked sockets, as vastly different as either end of the universe.

I walk up into the hills. What appears as a well-watered lawn from the sea below is merely a thorny green rampage upon sandy bedrock. I squat to let the land imprint itself upon me. The normally leafless *palo adán* plant is leafed from all of the recent moisture, cholla and pitaya (also called organ pipe) cacti beard a parched arroyo with verdancy, and *jejénes* crawl as thick as goosebumps on my arms. Looking over the semi-arid landscape of thorns to the sea, frigatebirds, pelicans, and gulls are hovering and plunging toward the turquoise waters like the *jejénes* working my flesh. The contrast of this cactied foreground against the bright sea is almost blinding. I know that the land is richer than it seems, and that the sea is half salt, but while scratching the bites that pebble my skin and pinching out a cholla spine, the sea beckons like an oasis.

I sprint back down past the wolf spider burrows; past a bull snake flattening like a rattler, past a small thicket of thorns, and past an old tire. I kick off my pants, fill my lungs, and dive into the water. While sitting on the bottom, it occurs to me that the sea is so entirely alien that we must quantify our world above by measuring its distance above "sea level."

Here, amid water-muffled surf sounding like pure white noise, it is nearly reincarnation. Here, below sea level, this blurry, fluid universe is so familiar, so compelling, that if my ancestors didn't once crawl from the sea, I will surely find my next life in its embryonic embrace. My skin will become scales, my arms fins, and my lungs gills.

For now, I am forced to kick and bob to the surface. It takes a conscious effort not to open my mouth and let the sea fill my thirst.

31

~~~~~~~~

Playing Fish

The spear—SOMETHING watching from beyond—
Cold-blooded and finned

We don fins, snorkels, and masks. Now that we are south of the turbulent tides and sediment of the northern gulf, we can explore the world below.

The water is 78.5 degrees Fahrenheit, several degrees cooler than San Felipe temperatures, twenty degrees cooler than the oceans of our own bodies. For a quick swim it's refreshing. Go for too long, though, and your body temperature drops, fingers tingle, and your heart stamps like a web press slamming out an extra edition.

I dive ten feet down. It's dark. Above, the sea's forehead is a pearly-white, waving, translucent skin—covering the amber body of day. Like looking out the end of an enormous dark tunnel.

I bob back to the surface and blow water out of the

snorkel as a surfacing vaquita would, sucking back in a long breath of plastic-tasting air.

The clicking of unseen shrimp comes to our ears as underwater castanets. A clam squeezes shut as I tickle it with my finger. A black shadow big as my chest darts back under a reef thirty feet away.

Deborah is shivering, so I follow her back to shore. As Deborah goes running down the beach, I reach into my bow compartment and pull out two fiberglass sticks. The business end has three sharpened metal prongs and a foot of surgical tubing to fasten around my wrist and provide propulsion. I screw the three-foot-long sections together and waddle back down into the water, pulling down my mask and flopping back in as if I'm Neptune remounting my throne.

This time the fish are behaving more flightily—whether it is due to my predatorily fast swimming, the long yellow spear in my hand, or the rev of my heartbeat—I may never know. They do.

Gaff-tailed pompano dart away and I loose one shot, missing by a league. Bass scoot warily along the bottom, hiding under rocks, seemingly aware of my needs. Three black damselfish are sitting damsels, tickling their silken fins against my arm: far too delicate to shoot.

Out where the reef drops off, something dark flashes by, *something* as unproportionate to me as I am to the puffer fish. I keep glancing seaward, half expecting it to rush me. Probably just a passing hammerhead, a bovine manta ray, or a man-sized grouper—watching me stalking its food. I try to suppress my doubts by concentrating on the hunt, telling myself that hammerheads, mantas, or groupers don't attack snorkelers. *Or do they?*

I shoot at three more bass. I release my grip halfway up the spear and the elasticity of the surgical tubing cocked against my wrist fires out the spear as a foaming missile; bass shimmy into holes and the metallic *chuunk* of spear against reef announces each miss.

Puffer fish hang like underwater hot-air balloons, oblivious to any predator hungry enough to bite and fill its mouth with venomous barbs. I again consider the slender damselfish, waving filmy fins against my mask, but spearing a damselfish would be like shooting a mourning dove at a bird feeder.

My whole body is quivering, so I hug myself, biting my lips against the cold.

I finally shoot at a spotted sand bass, hovering nearly invisible under my flipper against the reef, secure in its camouflage until the spear gushes through its tail. I kick back toward the shore, my legs and arms trembling with cold as a moray eel darts out—a giant brown mouth—caressing my spear and staring into my mask with yellow beady eyes, then abruptly wiggling back into a dark grotto, sparing the bleeding and writhing bass.

I point the spear in the direction of my travel toward shore so the momentum of the swim holds the bass tight against the prongs. I wonder if it feels any pain as I fin back past the damselfish, who, for once, part obligingly; past the dirigible-shaped, O-mouthed puffer; past a silver blur of pompano.

At shallow water, I stand up and hold the foot-long bass in one hand, and shaking against the cold, pull out the spear. The bass writhes violently in my hand, pierces my thumb with a sharp fin, then squirts back into the sea; I lunge for it and miss.

Three hours in the water without a wet suit is too much. A roaring fills my head and I can't hear what Deborah is saying as she passes a cup of tea too hot to touch my lips to. As I slide closer to the stove, she towels my goose-bumped legs with the dirty tee shirt. A jet comes soaring our way, so I point it out to Deborah, flashing birdlike against the setting sun, drawing closer without any noise, so I blink my eyes only to discover it is a frigatebird. Deborah forces me to drink the tea. My fingers feel afire against the cup so I drop it and get up, flinging arms and legs, trying to bring my core heat back up and thinking, through the dull cloud of a hypoxia headache, *my body temperature is more fish than man*. I ask Deborah to please help me take off my fins.

32

Enchanted Vagabonds

The Katzs, the Lambs—Sailing to Isla Espíritu Santo—Lamb's Believe It or Not stories—Emulating a child

San Evaristo Bay is blasted by a stiff north wind. Three sail-boats stalk and creak around their anchors like greyhounds waiting for their captains to slip the leash. Marie and Eran Katz invite us onboard the thirty-eight-foot *Shulamite* for fresh-squeezed *limonada* and oatmeal cookies.

The other yachtsmen are lofting cocktail glasses and play-ing stereos on their teaked yachts; their masts are strung with salad-bowl-sized satellite television dishes. The *Shulamite*—with its cement hull, rust stains, and austere fittings—is just the sort of working-class boat that Deborah and I prefer.

Marie, twenty-eight years old, is from Vancouver. Eran is twenty-nine, a former tank commander from Israel; he looks barely twenty. While bouncing their two-year-old son, Jordan, upon his lap, Eran grins so wide that he sheds another year or two.

They have lived for several years on *Shulamite.* We fall into easy rapport, due to the commonality of our journeys, but while we are sojourning two months, Eran and Marie have spent the last year on the Sea of Cortés.

The record of modern, seagoing adventurers in Mexico is scant, but the Katzs follow a long tradition of vagabonds. In October 1933, Ginger and Dana Lamb paddled out of San Diego in a sixteen-foot, combination kayak-canoe-sailboat named *Vagabunda.* Dana wrote a book about their passage, *Enchanted Vagabonds.* For the first two weeks, they claimed to dodge the Mexican and American navies while riding with clandestine rumrunners, delivering liquor to America during Prohibition. After paddling further south, Dana wrote that his "hands and wrists were torn to shreds" by a "huge," rabid coyote; Ginger saved her husband from rabies by plunging his hands into a scalding pot of iodized water.

Later, their rope allegedly broke while rappelling into an old volcano crater. They crawled around in darkness all afternoon until escaping out a fissure.

In Scammons Lagoon, a whale supposedly breached beneath their boat, lifting them into space. Dana wrote:

> I suppose we were just another barnacle to that whale, but he looked like the *Queen Mary* to us! Then the canoe started to volplane and pitched violently into the water. The whale's great tail—it seemed twenty feet across—hovered over us . . . and then came down. The canoe bounced into the air and we catapulted into the channel.

Enchanted Vagabonds is rife with shark stories. Sharks chased Ginger around in a whirlpool; Dana saved her by breaking the sail mast off the boat so she could climb back in. Weeks later, Dana shouted at Jaws, circling the boat: "He's trying to tip us over so he can get a square meal!" And while anchored off a Sea of Cortés island, Dana lanced "huge" sharks, until the water became "a carnage," and "looked like a fireworks display" of phosphorescence as the sharks devoured one another and bit the *Vagabunda.*

Eran and Marie once caught a four-foot-long blue shark on their fishing pole. The only "horror" they describe was the prospect of wasting the shark—since the shark swallowed Eran's last fishing lure, they gaffed it on board *Shulamite* instead of cutting the line, then killed it. They pulled out the lure, sawed off a few steaks, and found a hungry family so the shark wouldn't be wasted.

The Katzs invite us out sailing. After yarding up the anchor, mired deeply in sand, the wind pushes us southeast. Eran follows the same course that Spanish sailors logged in 1734 to rescue the beleaguered Jesuit Father Taraval, trapped with Fabian on Isla Espíritu Santo.

The Katzs judge the local culture just as the early Spanish did. Marie and Eran feel badgered by Mexicans motoring alongside the *Shulamite* in *pangas,* she says, "Trying to sell us cigarettes, cheese, and asking rudely for cold water even though we don't have a refrigerator."

Marie and Eran mention a lack of initiation in the Mexican culture, a dearth of curiosity, and general impoliteness. "You know," Eran says in his clipped English, "we believe that most Mexicans are honest, but they are unwilling to improve their lives by improving things."

"Improving what kind of things?" I ask.

"You know," Eran says, "things like cultivating date palms, growing vegetables, and cleaning up their villages."

I argue that Mexico's fatalistic culture separates us from its people, and that the perceived rudeness is probably due to the barrier of wealth separating a *panga pescador* from a yacht sailor. "I know this because Mexicans don't harass us poorer folk in our kayaks," I say.

Eran and Marie shake their heads. Marie says, "Mexicans are simply unintelligent and unwilling to ask the sort of questions people ask in so many other countries of the world, like Peru or Turkey."

After living in America for several years, the Katzs are also aghast at "how stupid most Americans are." It's the little things that bother Eran and Marie, such as people who don't understand how automobiles work. Eran and Marie believe that to make any contribution in this world, a person must be able to understand the basic concepts.

"Van Gogh was probably an idiot under the hood," I offer, "but look at the beauty he left the world by painting."

No reply. Marie still wants to prove her point: "Most Americans are so narrow-minded about geography that they don't even know where Libya is."

A quarter mile off, a whale rises, twice, like a rounded rubber atoll. A marlin splashes out of the water, fencing after its prey.

Marie tests me: "Do you know where Libya is?"

"Sure," I answer playfully, "it's in Asia."

Our vagabond forebears, Dana and Ginger, made three attempts to cross the Sea of Cortés. Their first crossing, paralleling our present course, was thwarted by a *chubasco*. They paddled back to the lee of an island and watched "mountains of water propelled by an eighty mile gale. . . ."

Dana had only one complaint about his wife's cooking: "the tough and leathery tortilla which of necessity was our only breadstuff had become a trifle monotonous." The word *leathery* is emphasized twice more; Ginger made a stack of these tortillas for their next crossing attempt. After sailing all day, they hit a log, rending a two-inch hole into their canvas canoe bottom (which sharks only scratched). Water could be heard "gurgling" into the boat. Dana wrote:

> We had ten minutes at the most before the canoe would sink. Something must be done right now. I

shouted to Ginger, "Throw in the tortillas!" Without
question she obeyed me. I grabbed the stack, and
one after another placed them in and over the hole.

Dana claims that the tortilla plug held until they paddled
back to their island early the next morning. He repaired the
hull.

Their third attempt at the hundred-mile crossing was successful. The Lambs continued paddling down mainland Mexico, blasting with their Luger and .22 automatic past "jungle
gangsters" and gunbattling carbine-wielding Indians in hol-
lowed-out log canoes. Dana wrestled alligators. Ginger rescued
her husband from quicksand. In the jungle, they ran from a
five-foot-wide, two-thousand-pound tapir, "like a hog whose
metamorphosis into an elephant has been arrested halfway."

With their pistols, they killed an eight-foot tiger. They
surfed a "forty-foot wave" into shore. They were stricken with
104-degree malarial fevers. Dana survived an attack of appen-
dicitis by lying on ice for ten days. Their boat was blown out
"toward China," twice, for several days at a time and they were
repeatedly thrown out into the maelstrom, persevering through
capsize and desperate swims and legions of yellow-bellied sea
snakes.

They finished traversing the Panama Canal in October
1936; *Enchanted Vagabonds* was published in 1938. Forty-eight
photographs (of the gunslingers poised with dead animals,
with smiling natives, and their sixteen-foot canoe) preface the
text, perhaps to show that Ginger and Dana—his thin-musta-
chioed face bears remarkable resemblance to Errol Flynn—appear to be stolid, no-nonsense, American adventure journalists
who wouldn't dupe the reader with any fish stories.

The Lambs did finger one bright garment of truth:

There was in this wilderness, a sense of peace and
freedom. We had ceased fretting over the future and
what tomorrow would bring. We lived in a timeless

world where each day was complete in itself and one accepted whatever it brought without cavilling.

Sixty years later, Eran and Jordan and I snatch at slippery, two-inch-long needlefish fingerlings, blazing like neon arrows with their glowing enzymes as they shoot out of the darkening waters and grease through our fingers. Jordan has been silently leaning his head on the dinghy pontoon for long minutes; I cup the phosphorescing water in my hands, blossoming sparks into the sea behind us. Jordan is contemplating the glowing water with wonder in his eyes. I suggest to Eran that time must seem immense to his son, that Jordan must perceive minutes like these as hours. Eran smiles as though he might burst with love.

"That's why Deb and I came here," I say. "We want to stretch time out and feel childlike about the world again. Like your son feels right now. You know what I mean?"

We both look at Jordan. "Yes," Eran says, "I know what you mean. But it's not the quantity of time you should look for. It's the quality."

Jordan lifts his blond curls up from the water, beams at Eran as if to say *You're right again, Dad,* and nods, sealing our pact.

33

Losing Paradise: Isla Espíritu Santo

Great blue heron—The marketing of an island—Sea lions of Los Islotes—Why kayakers avoid mangroves

On Isla Partida, a great blue heron stands statuesque beneath a jutting "beak" carved out of a sandstone cliff by wind and water. The bird could have alighted anywhere, but the narrow-shouldered heron—looking half Jesuit in its robed vestments—chose to land next to the sandstone beak and mimick it as if the landscape is alive. Goosebumps pickle my legs.

The islet next to Partida, Los Islotes, is a destination for sea lion boat cruises out of La Paz. Although boaters are prohibited from walking on the sea lion rookery, divers regularly come and swim with the sea lions; the Katzs often motor in to play with the pups.

Isla Espíritu Santo, separated from Isla Partida by a narrow cove or *caleta,* is a destination for yachters, kayakers, and anglers partly because of the unlikely grace of its sandstone walls. On one point, a pebble and boulder wall rises forty feet out of the water and melds into a smooth sandstone wall as abruptly as unkempt grass next to a cement sidewalk.

Isla Espíritu Santo is no more or less lovely than the many isolated and hard-to-approach landforms to the north. The difference is that kayaking outfitters have marketed Espíritu Santo like Yosemite, Niagara Falls, or Yellowstone. Eventually, the sheer weight of visitation will take its subtle but inexorable toll. The trash gets picked up, and tourists sing the so-called praises of "wilderness," yet irretrievable shards of beauty disappear like pottery being stolen from Indian ruins. Sea lions will swim off, birds will stop nesting, and oyster beds will be plucked barren. Paradise is lost here.

Every white-sand *caleta* we paddle into on Espíritu Santo is colonized by large guided groups of kayakers, escorted by *pangas* that carry the kayakers' tents, clothing, margarita, and culinary supplies. At Caleta Ballena, a forty-foot powerboat roars back to La Paz with a dozen kayaks strapped onto a roof looking like a hat rack.

The beaches are relatively spotless, due, no doubt, to the annual island cleanup sponsored by local outfitters. We settle for camping in an unoccupied mangrove *caleta,* dragging our boats a hundred yards up the tidal flats. The freshwater seepages and mangroves along saltwater are avoided by kayakers for some reason—probably bugs.

John Steinbeck wrote: "The roots gave off clicking sounds, and the odor was disgusting. We felt that we were watching something horrible. No one likes the mangroves."

At darkness the sea scurries under the mangroves and a ringtailed cat—like an anorexic raccoon—scurries into the cacti.

We snuggle close until midnight, when the breeze drops and the *jejénes* whining in our ears warn us to set up the tent, but the tiny bugs squeeze through holes in the screened walls. At dawn, a raven circles our tent and caws us awake—replete with welts and swollen eyelids.

We sprint from the tent with *jejénes* haloing us. This morning, even our sacred coffee ritual will be aborted; our eyes dart out to the only refuge: the sea. No biting bug in my experience rivals the *jejénes,* not even New England's blackflies, which give their victims the satisfaction of a confirmed, crunching kill beneath a slapped palm—unlike the invisible *jejénes.*

Packing is complicated because we have to scratch each new bite as we throw gear into aft and bow, eyes darting seaward. A fishing hook snags in Deborah's paddle jacket, requiring a delicate, surgical procedure to free it, using one hand for slapping and scratching.

We finally stop paddling out in bumpy waters and cool breezes beyond the fermented stink of mangroves and the flight range of *jejénes.* We claw our fiery flesh, and when cursing seems insufficient, I bellow on decibel par with the sea lion bulls of Los Islotes.

34

~~~~~~~~~~~~

Pearling

Ancient oyster eaters—Mother-of-pearl—The Yaqui divers—
Rape or disease?

Since Hernán Cortés passed Isla Espíritu Santo 457 years ago,
the shallow oyster waters surrounding the island have drawn
men with the fervor of Alaskan gold miners. Carbon dating of
oyster shell remains shows that a seven-thousand-year-old
knifeless people, before the Cave Painters, burned open oysters in fires, ate them, and ornamented themselves with the
charred pearls.

Seventeenth-century European pearlers depleted the sea's
shallow-water oysters. Throughout the eighteenth century, the
Jesuits forbade pearling, until the king forbade Jesuits on the
peninsula, and pearling resumed with a new passion. In the
1820s, as pearls became harder to find, two English speculators
arrived with prototypes of the diving bell, but both men
thought the Sea of Cortés pearl beds "exhausted."

In 1830, a French trader developed a market for the lus-
trous oyster shells, or mother-of-pearl, which were found in
great mounds along the shores of oyster grounds, shucked
aside by pearlers for nine hundred miles, from the cape to the
Colorado River. Eventually the demand for ivory-radiant pistol
or knife handles, belt buckles, or various jewelry made from
the shells overwhelmed even that of the pearls. From 1872 to
1873, 15,417 pesos worth of pearl shells and 51,000 pesos worth
of pearls were taken. In 1874, it grew to 57,065 pesos of shells,
with only 27,500 pesos of pearls harvested. And in 1875, 97,190
pesos worth of shells and 14,255 pesos worth of pearls were
taken from the Sea of Cortés.

In the mid–nineteenth century, La Paz entrepreneurs or
armadores hired Indians from Sonora on the mainland (the
original Californians were all dead) to dive for pearls and
shells, which the *armadores* sold at great profit to Europeans.
The Russians also created a competitive market for pearls, simultaneously buying up sea otter skins until the animal vanished from the sea.

Sonoran Yaquis recombed pearl beds and dove to previously unreachable depths. In 1849, a passing American tourist,
William Ryan, wrote about them diving where we're paddling:

> Thirty canoes, filled with divers, started with us, and
> in half an hour we were on the ground. Here the wa-
> ter was the most beautifully clear I ever saw. It was
> some four or five fathoms in depth, but so transparent
> that the pearly treasures in its bed were as plain to
> our sight as though air only separated them from us.
> The divers divested themselves of every particle of
> clothing, with the exception of a girdle tightly bound
> round their loins, and armed with nothing but a
> sharp-pointed stick, about a foot in length, used for
> the double purpose of fighting sharks and digging up
> the shell, they commenced their labours. Starting up
> suddenly on the gunwale of the boat, and giving a

shrill whistle, to expel the air from their lungs, with a dive as graceful as a dolphin's leap, they plunged into the water, and made a straight course for the bottom. The dive itself carried them about two fathoms downward, and every subsequent stroke one fathom. Arrived at the bottom, they commenced digging up the shell, and each one soon returned to the surface with an armful, which he threw into the boat, and they would dive again for a fresh load, and so they continued for nearly three hours, with scarcely a moment's intermission. Some brought up fish and sea-weed, others beautiful shells, and one fellow captured a small shark, which he threw into the boat, very much to the annoyance of us landsmen.

After the divers or *busos* could dive no more, they paddled their canoes to the beach and threw out their oysters. Half were piled up for the *armadores,* then opened with knives. The natives were watched "carefully," Ryan wrote, " . . . as some of them are very expert in suddenly swallowing any valuable pearl they may chance to find in the owner's pile." Sometimes a hundred oysters were opened without finding a pearl—created over a period of years when a sand grain inside the shell stimulates the production of the nacre coating.

Then the *busos* fell upon their own pile. The *armadores* traded the *busos's* pearls for liquor, chocolate, and to liquidate their room-and-board debts—at half the value of the pearl. The "black-looking" *busos* returned to their mainland shacks, to sup gruel and go blind with drink, until their labors were forgotten, and the *armadores* shook them awake for the next day's work—not dissimilar from the Alabaman cotton-picker slaves of the same era.

In 1857, the Governor of Baja California, José María Esteva, implemented far-sighted conservation. He divided the Sea of Cortés into four districts and allowed only one district a year to be worked by the pearlers; local judges enforced the rules and tried to seed new oysters in order to assure ongoing fertility for Mexico's pearling industry. But these regulations were impossible to enforce and like future fishing bans in the sea, officials took bribes and looked the other way.

An American and an Italian arrived in 1874 with eight improved diving suits and cleared $100,000 from May through October. Within a few years *armadores* trained Yaqui *busos* how to use the suits, and although many *busos* drowned or died from "the bends," they soon learned how to work beyond the suitless fifteen-fathom barrier. Treasures like Hernán Cortés's forty-two-hundred-peso pearl (appreciating tenfold after several centuries) were being pried out of 1880s oysters.

Sea of Cortés pearls were renowned as off-white pearls. North of Mulegé, pearls could "repeat the flesh-pink color of cloud pierced by the sun" (called "nacreous"), the blue of the sky, jet black, or more rarely, green.

The Mexican revolution in 1914 stopped the industry for a few years, but the Mangara Company kept its license until 1932 (President Francisco Madero had earlier talked the English company out of an exclusive license so that Mexico could eventually exploit its own resources). Attempts to cultivate pearl-bearing mollusks failed. Divers raked over every pearl-producing oyster bed in the sea—just like latter-day trawlers and long-liners.

Max Miller wrote about a visit to La Paz in 1941: "The pearl oysters suddenly all died within a single season not very long before my arrival. The beds all died at once, even those which were a hundred miles apart."

In the 1920s, Japanese cultured pearls—more consistently round and white—began to shut down the world's natural pearl fisheries. During the 1920s in America (the largest world buyer of pearls), there were several hundred natural-pearl dealers. By 1950, there were six; now there are none.

By 1940, a speculated disease, combined with overzealous harvesting, wiped out the entire population of pearl-producing oysters in the Sea of Cortés. Today in La Paz people still believe that Japan deliberately introduced a disease because pearls all mysteriously disappeared after the attack on Pearl Harbor— when Mexico forbade Japanese trawling in the Sea of Cortés.

As Deborah and I paddle away from Isla Espíritu Santo toward La Paz, frigatebirds roil an empty sky. The wind fills out the sea, blanketing the oyster beds below, nestled beneath brown waving fronds and fiddler crabs. If we cared to eat oysters, we would dive for them, even though the pearl-bearing mollusk no longer exists.

From an economic perspective, Mexico has only lost another industry and its revenues; from an environmental perspective, the demise of pearl oysters started the Sea of Cortés's exploitation. In the fathoms and years that separate our kayaks from Spanish soldiers and pearling entrepreneurs, the violation of Pericú and Yaqui were acts that no national treasury can repay—acts that continue to foment modern-day indigenes and leave Mexico perched on the brink of revolution.

35

⟿⟾

City of Peace: La Paz

Of Steinbeck and paceños—*Trying to touch ancient bones—Black yachts and sterilized harbors—Heavy metal Mexican marines*

We hitch a ride into the city on a shuttle bus of Canadian softball players dissing their "beaner" competition. La Paz's scarcity of tourists delights *paceños* (locals), who have a prospering economy (population 200,000) without too many gringos, allowing us to revel in tactile Mexico, bereft of the press of tee shirt shops and real estate offices found in other peninsular cities. Greasy fish tacos and cilantro permeate the breeze; a rooster crows from beyond a distant fence; disconsolate guitar music is plucked apart by the wind wafting in from the plaza.

At El Museo Antropología, I return to the exhibit with the

tawny, brittle-looking skeleton of an aboriginal in an open-air display. I pretend to be having trouble translating the Spanish placard, hoping that the guard will leave the room so that I might just once reach down and touch the bones of a Californian long extinct. But the florid-faced guard will not leave me alone; perhaps he knows that curious foreign hands like mine originally contaminated the Pericú.

After the sun sets it's a pleasant sixty-nine degrees, but we feel naked in short pants; *paceños* wear tight Levi's, long skirts, dress shirts, and patent leather shoes. The cars are all new and waxed and reverberating with Mexican music. Only a drunken mariachi, selling romantic songs, asks us to buy anything. Ice cream cones are more expensive than in Aspen, and all three shops along the harborside are bustling with *paceños*. The jewelry shops facing the sea are similarly busy, selling mother-of-pearl and cultured pearls from Japan.

Steinbeck is known for writing about Alta California, even though he was equally enchanted by Baja California—judging from his books championing the poor in *The Pearl* and his lyricism about La Paz in *The Log from the Sea of Cortez* ("Guaymas is busier, they say, and Mazatlan gayer, but La Paz is *antigua* [old world]"). In *The Log* he wrote:

> And we wondered why so much of the Gulf was familiar to us, why this town had a "home" feeling. We had never seen a town which even looked like La Paz, and yet coming to it was like returning rather than visiting. Some quality there in the whole Gulf trips a trigger of recognition so that in fantastic and exotic scenery one finds oneself nodding and saying inwardly, "Yes, I know." And on the shore the wild doves mourn in the evening and then there comes a pang, some kind of emotional jar, and a longing.

A Sylvester Stallone movie is held over in the nearby theater, alongside a *Rambo* parody and X-rated movies. Although the sea appears lucid under the *malecón* street lamps, we can smell sewage leaking into the bay. Over a hundred yachts are at anchor, hulls painted with an antifouling component to inhibit the growth of algae. The copper herbicide in the paint flecks off the boats and kills any bottom dwellers—effectively sterilizing the harbor.

A black yacht from Isla Espíritu Santo motors in. The Boston-accented woman onboard told us about catching a "shitload of fish" and claimed to "hate yachties." Her mast has the telltale satellite television dish halfway up, along with the prerequisite refrigerator, ice maker, and blender down in the cabin. Fifty-three years ago Steinbeck observed:

> [A] black yacht went by swiftly, and on her awninged after-deck ladies and gentlemen in white clothing sat comfortably. We saw they had tall cool drinks beside them and we hated them a little, for we were out of beer. And Tiny said fiercely, "Nobody but a pansy'd sail on a thing like that." And then more gently, "But I've never been sure I ain't queer."

We find a cheap *pensión* on a side street and try to scrub the sand off one another in the cold shower. As we scrawl out a market list, a mariachi band practices below our window and we breathe in the perfume of evening primrose knowing that Mexican music—with its bittersweet piercing lyrics and maudlin guitar riffs—will always remind us of the sea: how we watched its slow demise, how it brought us closer together.

We dance naked as Pericú beside the open window, unseen by the *músicos,* letting their sad medley into our room and dancing in a sea of desire so pure that it is untainted by time or cultural boundaries. Her skin smells of coconut and tastes of salt, and now as I brush fingers across her broad face with its strong chin I know how she feels: warm and secure and unalone, just as I feel. We have sacrificed everything to be alone together in this strange land, upon this Vermilion Sea. I could never have paddled so far without her.

I pick her up and she is lighter than my kayak and as we continue to dance—her legs wrapped around my waist, my arms akimbo—a sense of fluidity lifts us above our petty cares. We have lost the *weight*. Leaning with the waves. Carving into the wind. Coasting on the riptide.

The music stops sometime later. Yet in our heads this night it plays on with all the depth that both sorrow and joy can bring; it plays on and on and on; it plays on as waters inviolate.

We hitch back to our kayaks with an arm-straining duffel of groceries. Two twenty-year-old marines pick us up in a Camaro. They swig Gatorade, offer us cigarettes, and sing harmony to a Mexican ballad on their stereo.

Their innocent behavior contradicts that great beast machismo, but I can't help but wonder if they're singing for Deborah's benefit—if I were hitching alone, they would never have picked me up. Deborah is every hitchhiker's best companion in Mexico. Deborah is *una güera*.

They drop us at our *kayakos* and they wave coolly, Mexican style, holding their hands down. Their Camaro squeals out a long stripe of rubber as the navigator flips in a more recognizable tape and cranks up the volume, until the fading screams of Guns N' Roses is replaced by the preordained beat of the sea, breathing the ancient, impassioned song of our earth.

36

·~·~·~·×·~·~·~·

Stranded on the Point of the Dead

Capsize—Ed Abbey revisited—Desert wood rat—The nightmare wave hits—Defining love

Night blackens day and traps us alongside surf crashing on rock. We paddle back north a mile to an unprotected spit of sand, and the surf quiets. While I am investigating the landing, a sudden wave lifts me up and over a rocky shoal, spins me sideways, and before I can paddle brace, I am shoved face down into the water inside the breaking wave. I kick out of the boat, protecting my head with my hands as the sail mast breaks loose, clunks my face, and punches through the front bulkhead—flooding both the cockpit and the bow stowage. Now I'm mad.

I kick my "bathtub scow" and wrestle it to shore, straining my back. Deborah lands effortlessly.

I am upset more for being careless than I am about damaging the boat, bruising my face or pulling a back muscle. The headlamp battery is dead, but a sliver of moon casts our shadows onto the sand. It's fifty-five degrees and windy, so I pull on my fleece vest. Thinking that a fire will cheer me up, I spark some driftwood to life, and sit beside it, nestling my head between my knees, while Deborah scratches *jején* bites scabbing her legs.

A good repair job can salvage everything (including me), so I dig out our ten-pound repair kit, cut apart a Cordura water bag, and barge cement the waterproof Cordura over the torn kayak bulkhead. I flip the kayak over and apply epoxy to worn spots on the hull; pull apart the stove and ream out the gas pipe; duct tape driftwood cane over two broken tent poles; patch a leak on a dry bag; reepoxy the mast footing to the kayak floor; and screw a new bulb into Deborah's headlamp. Fixing things make me feel better and helps me sleep soundly.

Deborah threatens to leave the tent unless I hold her. So we cling as barnacles to a hull.

The wind comes out of the north and whips the water like a beater pulling up egg whites. I can feel the bite of winter on this wind, imagining the snow blanketing our Crested Butte home. Refracted swells from the Pacific collide against the wind sharply, so we keep our sails trimmed and consult the map carefully, memorizing each potential landing for twenty miles. We agree that if these winds don't relent soon, reaching the East Cape is the safest and most logical conclusion to our journey, rather than fighting into Los Cabos on Pacific swells.

A big needlefish is snatched by an osprey, its wings beating heavily, its prey curling in the talons and snapping crocodile jaws until the osprey drops the fish, shimmering like an electric blue pipe and dropping through a cloud of wheeling gulls, splashing back into the water. The osprey disappears into saguaro cacti.

Before landing on the protected beach inside Punta los

Muertos, the Point of the Dead, a six-pound jack crevalle dives to the bottom with my trolled lure, then comes straight up as fast as I can reel, plopping into my cockpit with a quick flip of the rod. Holding it down by the strange side spine with my fingers, I quickly punch the knife behind its eyes. The jack gives one final shiver, I let it go, then land the kayak.

I fillet the blood-dark meat in ceviche-sized chunks, mix in a can of salsa, the juice from two limes, a diced onion, then let it all marinate. After an hour, the lime has cooked the jack meat to a pasty brown and we eat with our fingers. It is sweet and tender and bursts in our mouths like biting into cherry tomatoes.

Waves thunder onto the beach. We pull our boats up again. The surf foams up the shore and bubbles into crab holes, tickling our faces with spray as the dark stain of water recedes and disappears back down toward the sea like high-speed movies of storm clouds racing over the desert. The normally placid waters of sunset are roiling our protected bay with a primal chaos unlike any event for the past 750 miles. The implosion of surf and riptide would pull us away if we stepped into it. We will stay put tomorrow.

The wind howls around the Point of the Dead, shaking our darkened tent. As I sleep, a dream comes about the author, Ed Abbey, sitting here on the beach advising me how to write my book. He laughs as the wind snaps three of our tent poles. The gray-bearded, vulture-beaked bard of the desert pounds the sand with his fist as he guzzles a can of Tecate and rails—in his distinctive, unemotional baritone—about the Mexicans and the Japanese raping the sea.

At first light I see tent poles jutting through ripstop nylon. Slowly and meticulously duct taping the broken aluminum poles together—being quiet so Deborah can sleep—I contemplate what Abbey would have written about this desert Polynesia. Four years ago I attended his sunrise memorial service in the Utah desert and watched the American flag mysteriously falling over, so Abbey's friend Doug Peacock hoisted it back up, holding his chest out and smiling. Barry Lopez stepped to the podium and a sudden gust of wind came out of the still sky and scattered Lopez's eulogy notes across the slickrock; most of the crowd thought Abbey was there, raising hell.

On the beach behind Punta los Muertos it occurs to me that I rejected writing a biography of Abbey and came here instead, a place that Abbey had been writing a book about before he died, lamenting the end of arid wilderness, living out the Richard Shelton poem —" . . . my desert, yours is the only death I cannot bear"—until Abbey's own premature death.

I ponder the bard of arid places while poking about the flotsam and jetsam, while torching burnable trash with my lighter, and while kicking past Tecate cans, empty liquor bottles, shoes, toilet paper, tire-tracked dunes, cans, a mattress, and broken glass. The soul of the land—call it the land's dignity—has been desecrated along this road-accessed, southern portion of the peninsula.

Abbey lived in a border town and had a tacit understanding of both desert life and Hispanic culture. Had he lived to finish his book he would surely have written that the Mexicans have committed "Chingar!" upon the peninsula; *chingar* originates from the conquest of Mexico and resonates with meanings, depending upon the inflection. Shouted disdainfully, it becomes a masculine verb implying rape and destruction.

I kick at a piece of abandoned muffler sticking out of a dune and shout once, "CHINGAR!" In a soon-to-be flooded refrigerator, embedded in the sand, a stiffened desert wood rat lies half dead with hunger. I offer the thumb-sized rat an open hand, which it refuses to climb aboard but bites on so tightly that I lift it out, suspended from my ring finger. Deborah doubles with laughter.

We feed it shards of cracker. "Ratly" romps around, more dog than rat. As the beach visibly steepens on the second morning from the pluck and whirl of the sea, the tiny creature sleeps in my pocket as if I am its marsupial parent; the sands retreat back into the sea; black winter clouds race south and the wind fills the void. Without actually touching the water, we come to understand the sea with new intimacy, watching it undress toward us minute by minute, hour by hour, day by day: the long, sweeping, slapping curlers, building and building into a deep roaring basso, then rolling and falling and exploding into spray; going quiet and building all over again. It's a dangerous hypnosis. Gaze too long into the abyss, Nietzsche said, and the abyss shall gaze into you.

On our third night at Punta los Muertos, still stranded by the thundering water, we are so mesmerized and acceptant of the sea's breakers that we don't bother moving our tent back again—we've already moved it back three times. At 5:16 A.M. the wave of my week-old nightmare hits the tent as we're sleeping and Deborah screams at the warm water flooding over our legs, and as the tent tugs quickly toward the sea and I sit up fumbling with the zipper, it feels as if we are driving through an avalanche but all the car doors are locked and even though the wave has retreated, she bats me aside, opening the zipper a long minute after the wave is gone.

I run down and grab a retreating pot. We pull the tent back forty yards. No more rogue waves come, but sleep is now impossible.

The wood rat has washed away.

We retreat deep into ourselves. We are in total isolation upon Punta los Muertos (the nearby dirt road must have washed out between here and the cape). We glance up to check the sea with the regularity of Friday afternoon factory workers watching the clock, while turning pages of a shared book. We are set afire by the story, which I perceive as a book of illuminating new ideas and Deborah perceives as a love story.

At the next page turning, Deborah asks, "What do you think the meaning of love is?" Our journey has been a gift of *unthinking,* a time in which we have quieted our minds and tried to exist in the here and now, as children do. We are not finding the answers to our marriage, but we are at least learning how to ask the questions. I hesitate.

Finally, I just say it, rather than thinking it: "Love is giving of yourself spiritually." By the quizzical tilt of her eyebrows, she needs more, so I continue, "And in a relationship with another person, it's giving with more and more devotion, until you begin to, as we do, share similar thoughts."

"I think love is an emotion," Deborah replies. I press her and she says it can't be told, but she will write it down for me in her journal.

Our differences, the differences that exist between every man and woman, confront us here more vividly than ever before in our lives. It is so easy to fall into the stupor of not understanding love, or putting love on hold until we can fulfill other passions—as in a career, as in writing a book, or as in . . . a long journey.

I have learned something about *us* during the last two months. Being surrounded by the wild tangle of singing shells and brackish water and infinite sky with your partner would either send you both scurrying home to territorial safety to avoid the issue of love, or would impel you to stay and deal with fear and uncertainty and your own intractable wills.

Here, we cling to each other, compete with one another, and skip that baffling word across the sea to each other like a life vest. Here, I feel as full and confused and impassioned as the storm waters reaching for our tent.

37

The Sea's Last Mantas

Riding a wild sea—Legends of man-eating devil fish—
Slaughter on a pristine beach

On the fourth day the wind dies just enough for us to leave Punta los Muertos. Multidirectional waves demand our concentration. Although I have overloaded my bow for stability, the shore-refracted waves are still picking up the bow and spinning me out. To keep terror at bay, I quiet my mind from all thought and focus upon the water as if it is a chess opponent from whom I have to anticipate every move. Deborah is just the opposite, talking about the book we're reading to dispel her fear.

I grunt and steer closer to shore. Like most men, I need to focus and concentrate when I'm scared.

"I just babble when I'm scared," I hear Deborah saying as I pull out of voice range. "Jon is probably thinking *shut up Deb*. But why won't you talk to me?"

"I just can't," I reply, "please let me deal with this water."

Three miles later we know that the water is too chaotic and unpredictable—we have to exit, quick. We come to the only protected landing for miles, a rock breakwater. The waves are exploding over the breakwater with uncanny resemblance to the race of snow avalanches: roaring white out over the green still water as if it were a stand of evergreen. As I pull forward and begin surfing in along the edge of the breakwater, I hear Deborah screaming at me because I can't talk to her—I need to stay focused: a wave furls me up and then in toward the calm lagoon of water, and just as I begin to feel a breeze on my beard, the boat gently settles into the lee of the breakwater, next to an anchored *panga*. Deborah joins me, her cheeks wet with fear. She narrows her eyes and pokes me in the chest, pushing my buttons, blaming me for her fear; I paddle away even though she needs a hug or consoling. I'm too shaken by the sea.

A jowled man meets me up on the beach and shows us a sheltered tent site. Although Mexicans are normally nonplussed, his *panga* has been docked for four days, so he regards us with a mixture of scorn and amazement—we are either very stupid to be out in such water, or very blessed. He leaves as suddenly and formally as he arrived.

Half an hour later, he comes back with a pot of greasy beef-and-jalapeño soup, a package of crackers, a lime, fresh-chopped cilantro and onion, a gallon of drinking water, spoons, bowls, and napkins. We both bow. It is Sunday and he leaves to rejoin his family. We bend our heads and sup without stopping, until the pot and bowls are empty.

In Bahía Ventana, we paddle up to a beach of gringo windsurfers—Germans, a Canadian, and Americans—all frustrated by the sudden calm. They want wind. We want tranquillity.

We meet a curly-haired fisherman, ten years younger than we are, selling fish to the windsurfers. Pablo smiles a lot.

Pablo recently caught a three-hundred-pound, eight-foot-

wide manta—commonly sold in "manta tacos" throughout
Mexico—but lately, he says, "the big ones aren't around" (mantas grow as wide as twenty feet). So Pablo catches smaller rays,
blue sharks, and, occasionally, hammerheads. He tells the
windsurfers that the sharks won't hurt them during the day, but
at night, sharks prowl.

The early legends about bovine-mannered mantas are
more hyperbolic than the fables about sharks (from the same
class as mantas, called Chondrichthyes), which rarely attack
fishermen here. In Obrigón's *Journey of the Flame,* the La Paz
Pearl Divers' Association was called "the Manta Feeders" because "so many pearl divers were eaten by mantas." During
Vizcaíno's 1602 journey, Antonio de la Ascensión wrote:

> The devil-fish are so large that one of them wrapped
> itself around the cable of the anchor-buoy with which
> the *Almiranta* was made fast, pulled it up and made
> off with it and the ship, so that it was necessary to kill
> it, but a large number of soldiers and sailors who
> were pulling it with strong ropes never succeeded in
> getting it out on land from the water.

Numerous early accounts claimed that the manta ("cloak"
in Spanish) wrapped its seventeen-foot wings around human
victims—"it has not grown so large without having previously
breakfasted on divers"—and killed victims by "grinding its flat
teeth as it eats," recounted Obrigón's biographer, Blanco. "Rare
indeed is the man who escapes with his life," wrote another
eighteenth-century Spanish journalist about his Sea of Cortés
voyage.

While paddling up the Sea of Cortés in 1934, Dana Lamb
claimed to have harpooned a giant manta from his sixteen-foot
canoe. After being pulled on a short "joyride," Lamb wrote that
the manta came under the canoe, beating the boat with its
wings: "We bounced round like a cork in a washing machine."
After they hit it with paddles, the manta towed them for two
miles, so fast that it "threw a spray ten feet on each side of us."

Eventually, Dana and Ginger Lamb dispatched it with their pistols, using what could only have been an unlimited supply of ammunition, given the repetitive descriptions of gunplay in *Enchanted Vagabonds*.

During Steinbeck's voyage six years later, his crew repeatedly tried to take a manta specimen, but every time Tiny harpooned one from their seventy-six-foot boat, the manta broke the line, or pulled away, leaving them with only a chunk of leathery flesh.

Even Steinbeck exaggerated about mantas. In a letter to his literary agent, Elizabeth Otis, written from the Sea of Cortés, he wrote, "And yesterday we were collecting in a tiny bay when a huge manta ray came in. He was about sixty feet across so we got out of the water fast."

The manta ray got named "devilfish" because of cephalic-horn fins, used to scoop plankton and small fish into its mouth. These cephalic fins enable mantas to grab anchor lines then swim up the cable and rake annoying parasites off the fins—perhaps also explaining why mantas jump out of the water. Just north of here, a diving journalist, Marty Snyderman, reported pulling off an embedded fisherman's rope from an eighteen-foot-wide manta's rostrum. Snyderman wrote:

> Whether the manta was grateful for our efforts and wanted to show its appreciation . . . I do not know. But it simply would not leave us alone. The ray constantly cut in front of us and then stalled as if to say, "grab me, grab me." On my first ride I climbed on near the surface and the ray quickly dived to a hundred feet. Then we were back near the surface to start a series of turns and dives in a display of aquatic gymnastics. . . . One episode took me near a small group of hammerheads. As we approached, the sharks spooked and bolted away. . . . All of us rode him over the next several days in a form of communication that is rarely enjoyed with wild animals.

On the eastern edge of Ventana Bay, Deborah and I paddle over to a shipwrecked steamer, shoved onto the ivory
sands by the northerlies. The water is transparent jade and as I
come to the stern of the shipwreck, five large and lifeless forms
appear on the tideline, clouded with *jejénes.* The air smells only
of salt, so the carnage is fresh. I jump out; they're mantas.

The wings of these five-foot-wide, several-hundred pound
beings have been skinned alive for meat—perhaps twenty
pounds worth per animal. The scene is remarkably familiar,
and when I recall all the fishermen who told me how prolific
the mantas *used* to be several years ago, it evokes the buffalo
herds inundating the vast American plains. Buffalo were occasionally skinned or selectively butchered for meat; more often
than not they were left untouched to rot in the sun.

The white-bellied, black-topped manta I crouch next to
was dumped here only hours ago. The meat from its wing bot-
toms was carved out with a sharp knife—the manta grunting
like a bear as chunks of flesh were ripped out and a reddened
fan of delicate bones was exposed to the merciless orb of sun.

Now the celphalic fins are stiff and its tiny eyes are brown stones. Deborah refuses to land and get any closer to the gore. Lifting my fingers from warm flesh, from spiny skin tough as leather, I know how the Sioux Indians felt, contemplating the last wasted carcasses of buffalo.

38

~~~⌒∙⌒~~~

Battling for the Californias

*Mexican-American War—An Unpeaceful Treaty—The Good,
the Bad, and the Filibusters—Those Alta Californians*

The rains have painted the East Cape with a riot of trumpet bushes, nightshades, desert lavenders, and scarlet poinsettias. America's emissary, Joel Poinsett, offered to buy Texas from Mexico in 1825 and he was laughed out of the country. He brought home only the colorful Mexican night-blooming flower, which he took the liberty of naming after himself.

Although Mexico had declared its independence from Spain in 1821, the peninsular people—a mixture of Europeans and mestizo—resisted being ruled by the new Mexican nation. The following year the English pirate, Lord Thomas Cochrane, sacked San José del Cabo and after *Bajacalifornios* repulsed his attack in Loreto, the peninsula sought protection by swearing allegiance to Mexico.

Over the next fifty years Mexico changed its government as many times. A dozen regimes were orchestrated by General Santa Anna—a name later given to the violent winds that sweep down the Sea of Cortés like invading armies. In 1836, Santa Anna's Napoleonic delusions of grandeur brought Mexico to its knees over the battle for Texas.

In 1846, a second emissary set out for Mexico with an offer to buy Alta and Baja California for 40 million dollars, and when Mexico refused to meet the emissary (having recently fought American troops again over the location of the Texas border), President Polk declared war.

The decisive battles of the Mexican-American War were fought on the mainland, while skirmishes occurred in Mulegé, La Paz, and San José. The United States planned to keep both Alta and Baja California, so when the army landed in La Paz in July 1847, it convinced the outpost of Mexican soldiers and influential citizens to become neutral—since they were now living on United States soil. Three months later, Captain Pinada arrived from the mainland and organized the nonneutral *Bajacalifornios* into a ragtag force, bearing muzzle loaders and machete's against the Americans.

Pinada recruited several hundred loyalists from all over the peninsula and after forcing the American army out of La Paz, Pinada's men marched against the invaders in Mulegé. The Mexicans fired cannons and drove an American warship out of the Rio Mulegé, buoying the *Bajacalifornios'* spirit. Later, they tore down the American flag in San José del Cabo—but American troops were so well entrenched there that a siege dragged on for months.

On February 2, 1848, a peace treaty was signed in mainland Mexico, but fighting continued on the isolated peninsula. In March, American soldiers captured Captain Pinada, and several days later, the remaining Mexican defenders were surrounded north of San José del Cabo; the war ended. Mexican irregulars were no match for American reinforcements and artillery.

The United States repeatedly proposed to keep both Californias, but Mexico successfully counterproposed that it would be a "great embarrassment" if Baja California was taken because the peninsula is so close to the Sonoran coast. As American troops withdrew from the peninsula to Monterey in September, they escorted more than three hundred neutral *Bajacalifornios* to America, lest they be executed by outraged Mexicans.

In 1853, Captain William Walker sailed out of San Francisco with a heavily armed company of filibusters. He arrived in La Paz on November 3, seized control, and declared himself president of Lower California. After skirmishing with Mexican forces and losing six of his men, Walker abandoned La Paz and killed Mexicans in several other peninsular cities before retreating to the United States.

Walker was then tried for violation of neutrality laws. The fact that he was acquitted reflected the sentiment of most Americans, particularly Alta Californians, about taking over Baja California. Two years later Walker was executed in Nicaragua during another filibuster attempt. And Santa Anna was deposed that year by Benito Juárez.

In 1874, the last nineteenth-century filibuster, Captain John Janes, visited San José del Cabo. After returning to the United States, the ex-politician composed militant rhetoric for newspapers, exhorting America to take the peninsula. Nothing came of it all, except a territorial pretense that Alta Californians continued to lord over the peninsula for a century, evident everywhere that we have paddled.

Today the narrow, hilly streets of San José del Cabo run between close-set Spanish colonial-style houses, tee shirt shops, and pricey restaurants. Flowers spice the air. Twenty thousand people live there. Downtown fences are painted by children with fish and birds and slogans about cleaning up the sea and picking up trash; the color green predominates. Even in this foreign country, one is left with a lingering impression, as distinct as the perfume of the poinsettias, that the environmental slogans are more imported American-style propaganda for tourists than actual doctrine of Mexico.

39

Journey's End

*Paunchy pilots of Punta Pescador—Feeling vital—Webster's
definition of filibuster—How to invest in the cape's
destruction—Our last dance*

By noon, the water is coming up at Punta Pescador again and
it's clear that paddling eight miles to Los Barriles will be no
mean trick. This sea is more suited to wind surfing than sea
kayaking.

We pull ashore beside yet another resort hotel and set up
our tent in the lee of a reef. Twenty-two, big American-style
homes have been built on the bluffs above the beach over the
last four years. We visit the hotel and contemplate eating Mexican buffet for thirty-five dollars each—not cheap, but we're
famished. While debating whether to return to the beach, we
lounge in front of the pelican-and-fish-tiled pool, among a
crowd of yacht captains and Los Angeles sportfishermen who
have dropped in for the night in their airplanes.

We can't help eavesdropping. One paunchy middle-ager is talking about how he never weighs anchor without two hundred pounds of ice onboard. At another table, someone warns a friend never to drive a car in Mexico. And when a third man comes to our table, having heard about our journey, he only asks if we've seen marlin.

At our favorite time of day—when most gringos are still asleep and yesterday's travails are forgotten—the water is disturbed. We beeline for Los Barriles. Two different Mexican *pangas* roar by, cutting their throttle and reducing the wake as we pass one another; I tip my hat. An hour later two gringos come by in a sunshaded powerboat without dropping their throttle a jot; we turn into their wake.

At midmorning, we are rocking in squirrely water alongside the resort of Los Barriles. I can usually *feel* when something will end, even though I don't actually *know,* so when I dip my feathered paddle into the inkwell of the sea, I close my eyes and savor it this last time: the paddle is impossibly light and I can feel the water move as if the blades are my hands. My back, shoulders (which stopped clicking two weeks ago), and arms feel pleasantly defined, as if I am always tilted toward dealing with some unforeseen calamity. My upper body has never be so finely tuned; I feel like a spring without the tension.

Too soon and we are standing on the beach with the kayaks listing on dry sand, as awkward as beached whales.

We wander Los Barriles for three days, making new friends and never lacking for dinner invitations or shelter from the sand mixing with wind and air down on the beach. The windsurfing community here and in Ventana—unlike most sportfishing communities we've seen—cherish their Mexican neighbors. They fish together, party together, and banter on the beach together. We never hear the derogatory *beaner.*

All day long, every day, we are pulled down to the riled water like filings drawn to an immense magnet. Even the wind-surfers talk us out of continuing in these Santa Anna winds, so we stare across the whitecaps and see our lives out there, made simple and pure. We have been brought closer to one another by the sea. It has scared us, in its power and in its crisis, so we have turned to each other in a way that might not otherwise have been possible. We stare out unspeaking as if we're not really going to leave. Here in this wild eternity of sea and sky we have been made whole and we don't want to leave and lose the wholeness, because going home will equal our demise, our inevitable divorce.

We don't understand the emotions welling up within us like the thickness of the flood tide—we are inclined to say that there is some connection between our own waters and that of the sea. When these moments of indulgence pass, they seem stupid and sentimental and unscientific. But everything in life must end and we can't deny our leaving any longer. We sit hunched over in the wind, stung by blowing sand, and filled with sadness so profound that we know what it must be to die.

On the last day of November we sell our kayaks to a wind-surfer and hitch the final hour to San José del Cabo. While our driver laments the loss of his windsurfing glory days as "King of the Los Barriles Beach," Deborah and I brood over our own passage. A tear runs warmly down my cheek, so I avert my head for privacy and catch it with my tongue: I am struck dumb by the common knowledge that our tears taste just like the sea.

Tourists throng the streets of San José del Cabo. Deborah and I feel their stares, because the journey has browned our skin, tightened our gazes, and given us a vitality that we're still trying to clarify. It might be that our vision is sharp from hours of staring out across the waters, looking for animals, and reading the sky. Or that we have smelled and heard and tasted things that we have never experienced. We are constantly hungry, but we can't eat as much as we used to; I feel somehow *full*. I feel sharpened. I feel quiet, as if mere conversation—except with Deborah—no longer matters. We have come to new levels of understanding after journeying eight hundred miles together. A smile can now equal what used to demand several declaratory sentences to one another, while the trip has shown us how much work, and communication, our marriage demanded of us.

The sea has shown us—through the wonders of an octopus's discerning eye, the stirring of water against shore, and the ever-changing light from the sky—a conviction, almost a faith, that the world is entirely too complex to be an accident. But thrusting forth the old saw—that God's face luminesces in nature—is a suspiciously familiar tune. Better to propose that the earth and its inhabitants are aqueous bodies all and if there is any truth to be found, we must first consult the waters that surround us. Our journey has shown us that the Sea of Cortés is one of the last pristine refuges and if we continue to consign it and its creatures to extinction, we will similarly doom all things aqueous and wild.

I arrive at the local place of worship, a church rebuilt in 1941 after the original Jesuit missions. It's all wrong. A lunette above the arched doorway features a tile mosaic of the Jesuit Father Tamaral being slain by Indians more Apache-looking— with feathered headbands and loincloths—than naked as the Pericú were. The message for all the worshipers who walk beneath the door is to pay homage to those pious men killed by the devilish heathens.

Across from the church in the shady town square, Plaza Mijares, stands a bust of Lieutenant José Antonio Mijares. No one stops. I run my fingers over cold bronze and wonder how many of the passing American tourists know that Mijares was killed by United States soldiers as he tried to storm their position and throw the invaders out of Mexico.

Today, militant couch potatoes—shrewdly passive Alta Californian filibusters—still mutter that "Lower" California should
belong to America. Filibusters is defined as "use of irregular or
obstructive tactics by a member of the minority" in Webster's
Unabridged English Dictionary, while the Spanish *filibustero* is
defined in various Spanish-English dictionaries as a "free-
booter" or "pirate."

Although nineteenth-century filibusters failed in their missions to retake the peninsula, there are now over a dozen real
estate offices in San José del Cabo.

Clean-cut young *Bajacalifornios* work for hire and offer
free condo tours to tourists, while the American realtors themselves snag passersby out in front of the realty offices. While
passing Century 21—Paradise Resorts, a realtor graciously in-
vites me in. I introduce myself as a kayaker rather than an investor. "With NAFTA getting passed," the man explains, "we're
just starting to have a resurgence in investment. We're at twenty
percent of what our market is going to be."

The realtor strides to a big map and excitedly draws a line
with his finger from the airport to the mountains, then north
along the coastline. He says, "The Mexican government has al-
located eleven billion to build a road from the airport to the
East Cape and all along the ocean. What does it mean? Increased property values."

He points again, east of the airport on the map, "You pave
this," he points to the perimeter of the Sea of Cortés: "you pave
that," he looks quizzically at me, "and what have you got?"

I shrug.

"Accessibility," he says. The realtor laments that the eigh-
teen-mile corridor between here and Cabo San Lucas, referred
to as Los Cabos, has only thirty-five hundred hotel rooms.
"That's the same as just one hotel in Las Vegas."

Century 21's "hottest" listing—or perhaps the only one that
a bearded, tousle-haired kayaker like myself could afford—is
eight miles east of here on a dirt road. There are 250 acres worth
of subdivided property; half-acre, oceanfront lots sell for

$150,000. "Twenty percent of what they will be," he reminds me. "Where does the sewage go?" I ask.

He shrugs.

"Is there any drinking water left?" He doesn't know.

Deborah and I walk south to make one final connection with our church, shining like a limitless mirage to the south, just beyond the high-rise hotels and the subterranean Rio San José—which ran underground even in Jesuit missionary days. The river estuary was the most reliable place for Spanish sailors and English pirates to take on freshwater. Now, mirroring the flow of progress in Baja California, its headwaters are heavily siphoned for irrigation and drinking water. Most farmers' crops would go dry before they dug deep enough to hit water. Except in flood.

Two weeks ago, a sudden rainstorm hit the outskirts of San José del Cabo and dumped nineteen inches of rain in as many hours. Several waterfront hotels were flooded and lost their beaches. Mexicans living in arroyo watersheds were washed to the Pacific by a wall of water that ripped out several-hundred-foot-wide chunks of highway. Locals tell us of bodies washing up on the beach and estimates of the people drowned—mostly arroyo shack dwellers—run as high as three hundred. But Mexico is tight-lipped about disasters in a tourist resort, and consequently, the United States media reports only a few dozen deaths. Until a few days ago, tourist jets to San José del Cabo were quietly rerouted to resorts on the mainland.

We commandeer two of the beach chairs at the Stouffer Presidente Hotel, pretending to be guests, even though we're shacked up at a flophouse across from Plaza Mijares. We stretch our legs and amble down the beach. Running is awkward. The muscles in my legs and the amplitude of my lungs have shrunk from the lack of aerobic exercise. However, forcing a million and eighty thousand paddle strokes over the last two months has given me a strange new clarity of purpose. It is like music playing in my head. I can will myself to do anything now so I find my stride simply by imagining my legs as paddles, pushing rhythmically against the water.

My pace slows, and Deborah picks it up. When she looks tired, I pull back. We don't speak because we can read one another's physical needs like the current rippling above the breakers; reading one another's emotions, however, is like interpreting wind against tide.

We flirt close to breakers powerful enough to snap kayaks in two, then sprint back upslope through briny mist, straining against the knee-high suck of the Pacific. We run for an hour, looking out to the ocean as if all the hotels and highways and beach walkers don't exist and we are Pericú out for an afternoon jaunt.

Up above the reach of most breakers, my bare foot grazes a striped snake—the yellow-bellied sea snake. We sprint up above high tide line and yank out a buried stick—one of hundreds recently flooded up on the beach—so the stranded snake can be pushed back in the ocean where it belongs. We return and the snake is gone, washed back by an unlikely wave.

"Deadly juju," as one San Diegoan described this snake to us nearly two months ago, but if we have learned anything since then, the yellow-bellied sea snake embodies the misrepresented American myths about Mexico. It is true that the species is the most common sea snake and that its neurotoxin is one of the deadliest poisons in the world. But no records exist of the snake ever envenomating anyone.

That night a band fills Plaza Mijares with music. The *músicos* alternate festive folk music with the sad, slow Mexican ballads. No gringos are dancing and the few who stop drift away when they don't hear "La Bamba" or recognizable mariachi tunes. The dancers are mestizos all, many of them dancing with inten-

sity furrowing their brows, clutching Tecate cans and one another as if the dance is all that exists and the music has become
their ocean of here and now. Deborah and I drift together as
neatly as slipping into a kayak, her breath against my chest and
my fingers similarly caressing her hair. Several *mujeres*—
wannabe *las güeras*—have dyed their hair blond. Cowboy-
shirted *viejos* and *muchachos,* stumbling *borrachos,* and *niñas*
in floral-print dresses all share the dance. Those with their eyes
open smile or nod whenever we make eye contact.

If no one is fooled by my Nordic wife, more than a few
people have mistaken my coffee-with-cream-skinned counte-
nance as *Bajacalifornio.* But I am a gringo, I will always be a
gringo, and my suburban roots cannot compare to people
perched upon the rim of poverty.

To learn what the Sea of Cortés really means to Mexico demands that you listen to the Mexicans. Their sporadically festive world is filled with sadness—a culture nearly subsumed by
fatalism and death, a culture that will turn the sea on edge until
all has spilled away.

Closing my eyes, I tune out the plaintive horn and soft guitar. I concentrate on the singer's language. Deborah and I circle
effortlessly with the innate and unforgettable rhythm of paddling, surrounding the two of us as tightly as a spray skirt. I
mouth the Spanish words and give myself to their music:

> I tell you friend
> Life's worth nothing
> Nothing is what life is worth
> Always begins with crying
> And crying its end
> That's why in this world
> I tell you friend
> Life is worth nothing.